GUPPY LOVE

Kids Can Press Ltd. acknowledges with appreciation the assistance of the Canada Council and the Ontario Arts Council in the production of this book.

Canadian Cataloguing in Publication Data

O'Keeffe, Frank
  Guppy love, or, The day the fish tank exploded

ISBN 0-921103-04-2

I. Title. II. Title: The day the fish tank exploded.

PS8579.K44G87 1986   jC813'.54   C86-093768-2
PZ7.054Gu 1986

Printed in Canada
Typeset by Alphabets
Design by Michael Solomon
Edited by Barbara Czarnecki

Kids Can Press Ltd., Toronto

86   0 9 8 7 6 5 4 3

GUPPY LOVE

or

The Day
the Fish Tank
Exploded

by

Frank O'Keeffe

Kids Can Press Ltd.
Toronto

To Class 4B 1984/85,
Pine Grove Elementary School,
Edson, Alberta

CHAPTER ONE

I fell in love for the first time the day the fish tank exploded.

It was recess. I had gone back to our classroom to get a cookie from my lunch kit. No one was supposed to be inside the school on nice days at recess, but I would only be a minute getting the cookie.

I heard the explosion just as I reached the classroom door. Kevin Windslow and Billy Pinchback rushed out, almost knocking me over, and fled down the hall.

Was it a bomb? Had they tried to blow up the school? I wouldn't put anything past them. Since school had begun, only two weeks before, they had been in trouble. They played tricks on kids as well as teachers. Only yesterday my friend Janet was embarrassed when her recorder made weird sounds in recorder class and Ms. Burton-Jones, the music teacher, got mad at her. Janet found sticky gum covering four of the holes on her recorder, and she suspected it was Kevin Windslow who'd done it. He sat behind her in class, and Janet's recorder was hanging in its case on the back of her chair.

Janet was furious and said, "I'll get him back— he's a big pest!"

I peered around the door. The room was empty. I stepped inside and a piece of glass scrunched under my shoe. What a mess! The floor was under water and a small wave was still coming towards the door. Our huge fish tank had burst, and the remains of it stood empty on the table at the back of the room. Bright green gravel was scattered around the room like confetti.

Where were the fish? I looked around anxiously for the four small guppies. That's all the fish we had so far. Mr. Martin had only set the tank up a few days before, and we were planning to get some more.

Nothing was moving in the remains of the bottom of the tank, but under Jennifer Mason's desk I thought I saw something jerk. I scooped up the guppy, which was flopping helplessly, and saw another at the same time. It had stopped flopping and seemed to be gasping.

Desperately I looked around for a container. The only thing in sight was Mr. Martin's coffee cup. I raced to his desk and grabbed it. It was half filled with cold coffee. There was no time to lose. There was no sink in the room to get water from.

I had to save the guppies, so I dropped the one in my hand into the cup. The coffee was cold and was made from water anyway, so it shouldn't hurt them, I thought.

I ran back to Jennifer Mason's desk and grabbed the second guppy I had seen. It was still gasping. I scrabbled at it and managed to pick it up, along with a few pieces of green gravel. I dropped the guppy and the gravel in the cup and looked around for the two missing guppies.

I was in luck—or they were. I found them moving slightly, trying to swim in the shallow water near the door. I dropped them into the cup too and set it back on Mr. Martin's desk. I raced out into the hall to find help.

I headed for the janitor's room, downstairs on the main floor, but before I got there, the bell rang for the end of recess and the kids started pouring in. I had to push through the kids, since I was going in the opposite direction. When I got to the janitor's room it was empty, so I headed down the next hall to the staff room. I wanted to find Mr. Martin and catch him before he got to class.

Too late! He was just disappearing up the stairs, hurrying to see why the kids were causing such a commotion. I pushed my way through another crowd of kids, trying to catch up with him, and got a kick on the ankle.

By the time I reached the classroom all the kids were in their desks except Billy Pinchback and

Kevin Windslow. They were standing, red-faced, explaining something to Mr. Martin. Kevin was saying, "We were only throwing a steely to each other—Billy missed it when I threw it to him, and it hit the fish tank."

Mr. Martin yelled, "Why were you in here? You know you're supposed to be outside at recess!" He lowered his voice, but he still sounded very angry. "Now go to the janitor's room and get a couple of mops and a pail and clean up this mess." He raised his voice again. "And be quick about it—go!"

Kevin and Billy fled like startled rabbits. The rest of the class sat deathly still and tried to keep their feet out of the water. We had never seen Mr. Martin so angry.

I nervously raised my hand to tell him about the fish.

"Yes, Natalie, what is it?" He still sounded exasperated.

"I put—," I began. Mr. Martin picked up his coffee cup and took a large mouthful. I stared, horrified.

Coffee and a guppy suddenly exploded from his mouth all over Tony Jackson who, unluckily for him, was sitting right in front of Mr. Martin. Tony looked startled. Mr. Martin looked in his cup and I ran forward to rescue a guppy for the second time. It had landed on Tony's mop of red hair. The class, stunned for a moment, not sure of what had happened, came to life and roared with laughter.

I picked the guppy off Tony's head and felt it wriggle in my hand. Mr. Martin started to laugh and passed me his cup. I put the guppy back into it and went back to my desk.

Mr. Martin kept saying, "Sorry, Tony," but he started laughing and couldn't stop. The class went into hysterics.

Mr. Martin bent over double and tried to ask, "Who put the guppies...ha, ha, ha," he roared again. "I'm sorry, Tony...here, have a paper towel."

He passed Tony a paper towel from the shelf, and Tony wiped the coffee off his head. Mr. Martin started laughing again, and at that moment, the door flew open. Ms. Beverley Burton-Jones, the music teacher, burst in.

"Mr. Martin," she began, "what on earth is going on? There is water dripping through the ceiling into my room."

"I'm sorry, Ms. Burton-Jones. We had an accident...ha, ha, ha." Mr. Martin couldn't control himself and started laughing again. He couldn't help it, and the class roared along with him.

"Really, this is too much." Ms. Burton-Jones stomped out, revealing a large damp spot on the rear of her pink slacks as she left.

My friend Tanya Sawatsky in 5A told me later: "We had just come into the music room, and Ms.

B.J. was standing on the little platform beside the piano. She clapped her hands and called in that high voice of hers, you know: 'Come along, children, don't dilly-dally,'" Tanya mimicked.

"Go on," I said.

"Well," Tanya chuckled, "we were standing in our places on the risers—I was next to Rita Watson. Ms. B.J. had just said that we were singing 'Michael, Row the Boat Ashore,' when I noticed a big drip coming from the ceiling. I nudged Rita and we tried not to laugh as the water kept hitting the piano stool." Tanya snorted and almost doubled up with laughter.

"What happened next—go on, go on," I urged.

"Well," Tanya went on laughing, "Ms. B.J. called out, 'Ready.' The piano stool was covered in water and there was a big pool on the floor around it—she hit the first note of the song and sat down on the stool at the same time." Tanya was laughing so hard that tears were rolling down her cheeks, and I was laughing too.

"What happened next? Stop laughing," I laughed, "and tell me."

"Ms. B.J. ..." Tanya howled, unable to control herself. "Ms. B.J. shrieked, the piano crashed, and she leaped off the stool. Her bottom—it was hilarious."

"You're making it up," I snorted.

"No, no, it's true. Her bottom was soaked in water, and while she stood there looking at the stool, another drip hit her on the head. The class went wild, and then Ms. B.J. stomped out." Tanya broke up again with laughter. "Gee, it was funny."

Billy and Kevin arrived with the mops and pail and set about cleaning up the floor. Mr. Martin got himself and the class under control, although occasionally he would start to snicker. Once or twice there were a few outbreaks of laughter.

Billy and Kevin couldn't understand why everyone was laughing, but they were glad Mr. Martin seemed in such a good mood.

Mr. Martin said, "Now who rescued the fish?" He looked at me expectantly and I raised my hand.

"I couldn't find anything to put them in," I said. "I thought they would die and I figured since the coffee was cold, it wouldn't do them any harm."

The class snickered, but Mr. Martin frowned and said, "Settle down! That was quick thinking, Natalie. Let's see if we can find something more appropriate for the guppies."

He went to the cupboard and found a large tin. "Here, Natalie. Get some water in this, please, and we'll dump the fish into it."

Billy and Kevin had most of the water mopped up by then and Mr. Martin sent Billy to get a broom and dustpan to sweep up the gravel and glass.

I went to the drinking fountain, thankful that Mr. Martin hadn't asked why I was in the room at recess. I brought back the tin with the water, and Mr. Martin scooped the guppies into it with only a little coffee.

"Well, they're still alive—thanks to you, Natalie."

I glowed.

"Now I must go and apologize to Ms. Burton-Jones, so please, while I'm gone, read silently. And no noise!" He winked at me as he left the room.

He was the first man teacher I'd ever had up till that year, which was Grade 5 at Elmwood Elementary. Mr. Martin was a new teacher in our school. I was glad I was in his class and so was Janet Sullivan, my best friend.

I guess the fact that he could make me laugh was what made me really like him. He told funny stories and was always coming up with bits of odd information that were interesting, like "Did you know that when you sneeze, the sneeze shoots out your nose at 160 kilometres per hour?"

I didn't fall in love with him until I rescued the guppies—though I don't think I realized it then.

He wasn't what you'd call good-looking, or what Janet would call "real cute," but there was something about him I can't describe. He was slim. He had dark hair, fairly long, and a dark moustache.

I would have died if anyone else had found out how I felt about him. I didn't even dare tell my best friend Janet. She wouldn't have understood anyway.

She would have said, "How could you fall in love with a teacher?!" Janet said she was going to marry a TV star.

Janet often expressed her opinions about teachers. In her opinion, most of them were mean. I thought some of them were very nice. Janet, however, felt you had to be against teachers on principle. They were adults, and adults didn't want you to have fun.

She would also have said, "In love with Mr. Martin—but he's so old!"

Janet thought most boys, except one or two, were gross and show-offs, and so did I, as a matter of fact. But she'd never understand falling in love with someone so old. I thought she wouldn't anyway, but I could have been wrong.

The next Friday we had Student of the Week awards in each class. This was going to be the first award of the year, and it was to be given to the winning student for good citizenship. I think that means doing good and helping people out.

Mr. Martin explained the award to the class and then said, "For showing such great initiative in rescuing our guppies, the award goes to Natalie Webster." The guppies I'd rescued were now in a smaller tank at the back of the room.

The class clapped and I went up to get my certificate. Mr. Martin shook my hand when he gave it to me and said, "Congratulations, Natalie." I blushed. As I went back to my desk Janet gave me one of her secret signs that meant, "I know whose pet you are—shame, shame," but I didn't care.

I've heard about women falling in love with older men. I've sneaked a look at some of the paperbacks my mother sometimes reads. Often they have women in their twenties falling in love with men over forty—real mushy stuff—but this was ridiculous! I'm only in Grade 5. Who ever heard of a ten-year-old, going on eleven, falling in love with her teacher who is really old—at least thirty-five, maybe even more.

I hardly remember riding home on the school bus that Friday. I felt like Cinderella riding in the golden coach to the ball. I stared out the window and daydreamed. I was still daydreaming when the kids all yelled at me because the bus driver had stopped at my driveway and I hadn't noticed.

I ran down the driveway of our farm, where I lived with my mom. My dad had died in an accident four years ago and Mom had decided to keep our farm rather than sell it. She'd got some life insurance money when Dad died, and although we could have sold the farm and moved to town, Mom wanted to stay. She liked the country life and had decided "to try to make a go of the farm," as she put it. Dad wouldn't have wanted to sell, and Mom knew quite a bit about farming because she had worked with Dad all the time. I enjoyed the country too, and I helped Mom with the chores, like feeding the chickens and the cattle, although I wasn't too fussy about cleaning out the barn. We also kept a few hives of bees, and I helped Mom with those too. I had my own bee suit so I wouldn't get stung. We extracted our honey and sold some along with our eggs at the local farmers' market.

Mom was in the kitchen when I went in, and I smelled the warm, spicy smell of my favourite cookies.

"Hi, Mom, I'm home. Guess what I won?"

Mom smiled. "Hi, what? Tell me."

I showed her my certificate and explained the award. I'd told her all about the guppies the day it happened.

She hugged me and said, "I'm very pleased for you. That's wonderful. We'll have to frame your certificate and hang it in your bedroom. I'll have to meet this Mr. Martin of yours. He seems like a very nice man. You certainly seem to like him.

"Now get changed, and after you feed the chickens and collect the eggs, come and have a cookie," Mom said. "They'll be ready in another minute. They're your favourite."

CHAPTER TWO

I couldn't wait for the weekend to go by. First I wanted to get back to school. I'd never felt like this before. Don't get me wrong, I like school, but this was different. I also enjoyed the weekends at home and I never felt too upset if I missed a day or two when I was sick.

The second reason I wanted the weekend to go quickly was that I was going to see Mr. Martin again Monday night. I had persuaded Mom to take me with her to Meet the Teacher Night.

Her only comment when I asked her was, "When I took you to Meet the Teacher Night in Grade 4, you were bored and couldn't wait to get home. What's the attraction?"

"Um...I think Janet is going too," I said. I knew it was a lie, but it was only a small one and anyway you never could tell. Janet might show up with her mother. That is, if the movie she told me she was going to see was cancelled or the theatre burned down.

Monday finally came and I had a pretty good day. Nothing unusual happened, but I was excited because I knew I was going to see him again that night.

After school I helped Mom with the chores. We had supper and got ready to go to the meeting. I combed my hair about five times, trying to get it to look good, and Mom was ready before me— something that had never happened before. "Your hair looks fine," she said as she saw me looking at it in the hall mirror and adjusting it over my left eye. "I almost think you must have a boyfriend."

I blushed and said, "Oh barf," my usual response to something I considered gross. A boyfriend was bad enough. I couldn't let her know I'd fallen in love with my teacher. She'd never understand.

We arrived just before the meeting began in the school gym. Mr. Stanley, our principal, welcomed everyone and said something about the school's program and Elmwood's school spirit, and how the teaching staff would make every effort to make sure that all students at Elmwood had a learning experience that was enjoyable.

He then went over some of the school rules, but he didn't mention any rules about falling in love with your teacher. He listed the rules about chewing gum, being absent (don't forget to send a note with your child when he or she comes back to school), the times school started and ended, lunchroom rules, and visits by the school nurse (could she tell I was in love by checking my pulse, I wondered).

"I don't see Janet here," Mom whispered to me.

"No," I said. "I guess she decided not to come."

"Her mother is sitting in the front row," Mom continued.

"Oh yeah." Oh darn! I thought. I hope Mom doesn't say anything to Janet's mom about me expecting to see Janet here. She would be sure to tell Janet. Janet would stare at me curiously in school tomorrow and say, "What's the matter with you? I told you I was going to see *The Revenge of the Sasquatch* with my brother. Who'd want to go to a boring old Meet the Teacher meeting. Boring!" And she would ask, "Why did you go?"

Mr. Stanley finished his little speech and began to introduce the teachers. When Mr. Martin was introduced and he stood up, I poked Mom in the ribs and whispered, "He's my teacher."

"Oh yes," Mom said. "He looks very nice."

I looked at him all the time the other teachers were being introduced and he smiled at me. I was pleased and I blushed, and then I turned and found Mom was also looking in his direction. I hoped she hadn't noticed me staring at him.

After the introductions were over, Mr. Stanley said, "Now we would like to elect our Parent-Teacher Committee for the next year. We must elect a president, vice-president, and secretary. Are there any nominations for president?" One or two people were nominated but they said they couldn't take on the job and gave some excuse.

Mr. Stanley then said, "Would anyone like to volunteer?" There was silence for a few moments, and then I nearly fell off my chair when Mom stood up.

"I'm Mrs. Webster," she said. "I would be willing to give it a try, but I'm not sure what I'd be expected to do."

I stared at my mom, who was already so busy trying to keep our small farm going, and who always said she had no time for anything else. What had got into her?

Mr. Stanley said, "Thank you, Mrs. Webster," and went on to explain that the job of president wasn't that hard and he would be happy to help all he could. Mom was chosen right away because no one else volunteered, and everyone applauded.

"Now that we have a president," Mr. Stanley continued, "are there any volunteers for vice-president?" Another lady stood up and introduced herself as Mrs. Zaretsky, and she got the job. The job of secretary was accepted by a Mr. Carlson.

Mr. Stanley then announced, "I would like

everyone to stay and help themselves to coffee and doughnuts and chat with the teachers. Could I please meet with the new Parent-Teacher Committee for a few minutes?'' Everyone stood up and headed for the coffee.

"Hi, Natalie.'' He was standing beside me, looking down at me. I leaped off my chair and stood up.

"Oh hi, Mr. Martin.'' Gee, I thought, I'm awful short. I only come up to just above his elbow.

"You look different tonight," he said. "I'm not sure what it is.''

Different!? What did he mean, different? Different than what? I didn't want to look different. Frogs in science class look different. I wanted to look attractive.

"I know what it is," he said. "It's your hair. It's different.''

Oh no! I thought. It's standing up on end again. I forced a smile, feeling really dumb, and resisted an urge to put my hand on my hair to check it.

"It's pretty," he said.

"Thanks," I mumbled. "Are we going to have any tests tomorrow?'' What a klutz! I thought, almost kicking myself. He says I'm pretty, and all I can think of to say is something dumb like that.

"No, I hadn't planned on any," he said.

Mom was standing beside us. "Hi! I'm Natalie's mother," she said.

Mr. Martin shook Mom's hand and smiled. "I'm

pleased to meet you. I hope Natalie is enjoying school."

"Yes, she is," Mom said. "At least she hasn't complained." She smiled down at me. "Would you like to go and get a doughnut, Natalie?"

I knew I was getting the brush-off, but I said, "OK," and went in search of the doughnuts. There I met Kevin Windslow clutching one in each hand. He'd taken a bite out of each of them. His pockets bulged suspiciously.

"Hi, Nat," he said. "How ya doin'? Wanna doughnut?" He nodded towards the box in front of him. "The chocolate ones are good."

I hated it when he called me Nat. He'd started calling me that in Grade 3 after we'd read a poem about a gnat, which turned out to be a kind of bug, like a mosquito.

I picked up a doughnut and a paper napkin. I left Kevin stuffing his face with the doughnuts and hurried back towards Mr. Martin, but he was surrounded by three or four parents. Mom was talking to Janet's mother.

"Oh, there you are, Natalie. Mrs. Sullivan was telling me that Janet decided to go to a movie."

"Oh," I said.

"Well," said Mom. "I guess we should be going soon—it's just about your bedtime and the school bus comes early in the morning." We said good-bye to Janet's mom, and as we were going out Mr. Martin waved at us. Mom waved back.

On the way home in the car I asked, "How come you volunteered, Mom—you know, to be the head of the committee?"

"Well, I thought it would be nice to find out a bit more about what goes on in your school and maybe have some say in how things are done. Nobody else seemed willing to volunteer, so I did."

"But you always say you never have enough time to do the things you want to do," I said. "Like that weaving you wanted to finish or that dress you started sewing."

"Well, I'll find the time, and anyway, there won't be a lot to do, just an occasional meeting, according to Mr. Stanley," Mom answered.

I said nothing. Mom had hardly gone anywhere or done anything since Dad died over four years ago.

I remember how we cried and held each other when it happened. I was only six then, but I remember Mom telling me that I had to try to be very brave and so did she. Then she told me Dad had been killed in a car accident.

We had both cried a lot, and somehow I knew Mom needed my help. I had tried to cheer her up when I came home from school each day and I knew she'd been crying. I had only just started school, and I had lots to tell her about what happened there. The farm kept us both busy, and Mom hardly ever went out anywhere. I think she hated to leave me. Gradually, however, she began to accept invitations from neighbours and went to one or two parties. She sometimes visited Janet's parents, because Janet's mother had been a friend of hers for a long time.

As I got older she realized, I think, that I was capable of doing things by myself and she encouraged me. She sometimes left me by myself for a short while to go to a coffee party at a neighbour's, but she never went out on dates. If she had to go out at night Mrs. Stevenson, our neighbour, came in to stay with me.

As we drove into our driveway, Mom said, "I saw you talking to a boy over by the doughnuts. Was he the one you spent so much time on your hair for?" Her eyes twinkled.

"Oh, Mother," I said. "You've got to be kidding. That was Kevin Windslow."

"Oh, so that was Kevin, was it?" Mom laughed. I'd told her all about him and Billy and what pests they were.

"It's too bad Janet didn't go to the meeting. I hope you weren't too bored."

"It was OK," I said.

CHAPTER THREE

Next day I had just stepped off the school bus when Janet yelled, "Hey, Natalie! I went to a great movie last night—you should have seen it. The Sasquatch was gross—he stomped on this car and squashed all the people inside—really neat."

"Sounds great," I said.

"My mom said you went to the meeting last night—boring, eh?"

I nodded. "Yeah, but they had great chocolate doughnuts, and besides, there wasn't anything good on TV. Mom didn't want to leave me at home alone," I lied.

Luckily Jill Lansbury came up then and started telling us about her sister's boyfriend and how she'd caught them smooching on the couch in their den. Janet was more interested in this. She forgot about me and the reasons why I would go to a boring meeting.

We went in and hung up our coats and put our lunch kits on the shelf in our room. Mr. Martin wasn't in the room yet. He was probably in the staff room with the other teachers, having coffee. Jill Lansbury was still going on about her sister and her boyfriend and was now retelling the story to a larger group.

I glanced up and to my horror saw on the blackboard, printed in big chalk capitals, "N.W. LOVES MR. M." As I ran to the board I saw Kevin and Billy smirking.

"Hey, Nat," Kevin called. "How come it says that you love Mr. M.?"

"Did you do that?" I said, my face flaming.

I grabbed the eraser and began to frantically erase the printing as Billy yelled, "Hey, look everybody!" and pointed to the board.

Just then Mr. Martin walked in. "What's going on?" he said. He looked at Billy and Kevin and then at me. I finished erasing and put the eraser back on the blackboard ledge and, with what I'm sure was a beet-red face, walked back to my desk.

The bell rang and Mr. Martin said, "OK, everyone. Sit down." Another day began. I was furious with Kevin and Billy and vowed to pay them back. How did they know I was in love with Mr. Martin? Was it a lucky guess on their part? Or were they just being smart, I wondered.

After announcements Mr. Martin called the roll and we started arithmetic. I don't really like arithmetic. It's not my favourite subject, and I guess I wasn't concentrating on what Mr. Martin was saying. I was still mad at Kevin and Billy.

"Natalie," Mr. Martin said. I looked up, startled, and I had a sneaking suspicion that he had asked me a question.

"Well, Natalie?" he asked again. Everyone was staring at me.

"I'm sorry," I stammered. "I wasn't listening."

"Well, try to pay attention," he said. "I was asking you if you could tell us how you would do this question I've written on the board."

I blinked. I hadn't seen him write anything on the board. It was a multiplication question—678 x 289. I could do it, all right, but I was too surprised and embarrassed.

Mr. Martin got tired of waiting for me, I guess, because he said, "OK, everyone. Watch while I do it." I sighed. Off the hook. I thought for a minute he was going to ask me to come up to the board and do it, but he was just giving an example.

The rest of the day went on as usual. I brightened up and felt great when, during our phys ed period, I managed to crack Kevin on the knuckles with my floor hockey stick when we both ran for the puck. He yelled and blew on his fingers, and although it was an accident, I felt good about it— like I'd paid him back.

The next day, however, there was another embarrassment. Mr. Martin was introducing a new story from our reader and was going over some of the harder words before teaching the story.

"Who can tell me what lopsided means?" he asked.

My hand shot up and when he said, "Yes, Natalie," I blurted out without thinking: "Dolly Parton."

The class tittered and I thought I saw a small smile cross Mr. Martin's face for a second.

"Dolly Parton?" he asked.

"Well, yeah," I blurted again. "You know—her breasts." The class roared, and this time Mr. Martin could not control his smile. It broadened into a grin.

Oh no! What am I saying? I thought. How can I mention breasts in front of everyone, and especially Mr. Martin? He was probably as embarrassed as I was.

He seemed to be waiting for further information, and the laughter had stopped.

"Well, that's what my mom says," I finished lamely. The class chuckled again and Mr. Martin told them to settle down.

He smiled at me and said, "I expect your mother may have meant 'top-heavy.'"

I shrugged. I wasn't going to say anything else and make things worse. But I knew what my mom had said—so either Dolly Parton was lopsided, or my mom got the meaning of the word wrong. Whatever, I wasn't going to make my mom look dumb and embarrass myself further.

Some of my embarrassment was relieved when a few minutes later Jimmy Hoover said eavesdropping was stuff you put around roofs, and Lisa Zuckerman said a spout was a husband or a wife. The class laughed at each blunder, but mine was the biggest and the one they remembered. "Lopsided" became an in word in our class for a few days, and "Dolly Partons" became a code word for breasts.

A few days later my mom went to her first school committee meeting. I was in bed when she got home, but she told me the next day at breakfast that the committee was going to plan an adventure playground for our school since there wasn't much for us to play on at recess and lunchtime.

"Sounds great," I said. "When will it be built?"

"Well, there's lots to do first. We have to decide what we want to build and we'll get some ideas from you kids too, as soon as we get some plans. We'll build a model of the playground. Then we'll have to get permission from the school board—and some money," she went on. "We'll get volunteers to build it and raise some money ourselves too. Oh, by the way, your teacher, Mr. Martin, is on the committee. He's really nice."

There was something about the way she said it

that should have warned me, but just then I dug my spoon into the grapefruit I was eating and squirted grapefruit juice in my eye. It really stung. I went to school that morning looking like I had a bad case of pinkeye, like one of our cows got that summer. I had to explain to the kids in school over and over again what had happened. Even Mr. Martin asked me about it. I was so embarrassed! I was sure he thought it was infected, but he didn't send me to the school nurse or anything to have it checked out, so I guess he believed me.

A month had gone by and I still felt the same way about him. It must be the real thing, I thought. It's lasted so long, and I still feel the same. Mr. Martin noticed it too. He spoke to me about it when I sat beside his desk, when he was going over my creative writing story. Well, he didn't actually come right out and ask me if I was in love with him. He was more tactful than that. He just said he'd noticed that I'd been doing a bit of daydreaming lately and had a sort of faraway look at times. He asked me if anything was wrong and I said, "No, no... Nothing." He went on reading my story. I liked his aftershave. It smelled like cloves. I like cloves.

They remind me of far-off romantic tropical islands. I could see us now on our honeymoon. The warm sun, the sound of the waves, the palm trees, the white sand, our own private island. I had a beautiful tan—we both had—and I was wearing that daring swimsuit I'd pointed out to Mom in the Sears catalogue, the one she said I wasn't old enough to wear. We lay on our beach towels and around us was the spicy smell of cloves.

I guess I must have got that dreamy look on my face because the next thing I knew he was staring at me as he repeated my name. My mind was still on that tropical beach when he underlined a sentence in my story that didn't make sense.

"Look at this," he said.

I stared at the sentence in horror. Had I written that? I silently read the words again: "When I opened the refrigerator door, he sat there, smiling at me, looking so good I wanted to kiss him."

"It's a perfectly good sentence," he said, "but who are you talking about? You said here you went to the refrigerator to get a glass of milk."

"I don't know," I said. "I must have been day-dreaming." I read the next sentence. "I poured the milk into a glass and drank about half of it in one gulp!"

I thought quickly. "I guess I meant that I was so thirsty and the milk looked so good. Yeah, that's it," I said. "It should be, 'When I opened the refrigerator door, the milk sat there looking so good I wanted to kiss it.' That's what I meant to write."

"Hmm," Mr. Martin said. "Well, try to keep your mind on your work. Now go back to your seat." He called Michael Collins up next.

When I sat down at my desk, Janet had a strange look on her face and she mouthed at me: "What's going on?"

I shook my head, not wanting to explain what had happened.

At recess she jumped me right away. "What were you doing up at Mr. Martin's desk? By the look on your face you were in never-never land or had just won Super Loto. He was staring at you for ages before you woke up."

"I was just sleepy, I guess. I was daydreaming and didn't hear what he said."

That was a close one, I thought. Other people are beginning to notice too. If Janet catches on.... "Let's play hopscotch," I said, wanting to change the subject.

It worked. "OK," Janet agreed, "but I get to go first." I didn't argue.

"How's that playground idea your mom's working on? When will it be ready?" she asked.

"I don't know," I said. "They have to make a model of it first."

"Well, I hope it's soon. I get tired of hopscotch. It would sure be nice to have slides and climbers and all for a change."

My mom had been to three meetings already, and I had seen drawings of some of the things they were considering. The rest of the committee were helping Mom get everything organized. She'd told me they'd make the model soon and take it to the school to see what the kids thought about it and to ask the kids for suggestions.

"You should see the new Bruce Springsteen poster I've got," Janet said as she threw the rock onto the hopscotch game. "It's hanging right over my bed on the ceiling so I can look at him when I'm lying down. I love Bruce Springsteen," she drooled as she hopped around.

I don't think she really meant it. Being in love with Bruce Springsteen, I mean. I didn't think you could fall in love with someone on a poster or on TV. But I wondered what she'd say if I told her I had Mr. Martin's photo in the bottom drawer of my bureau by my bed. I'd cut it out of the class photo that we'd got a week ago. It looked a bit weird because I'd had to cut around Jason Hopkins and Marie Lacroix, who were standing in front of Mr. Martin. When I cut them out, the part of Mr. Martin's body that was left looked really skinny. Only his head looked normal. I thought of cutting his head off and sticking it to a piece of black paper. But who ever heard of anyone keeping a picture of only a head?

It was my turn with the rock, since Janet had stepped on a line. But just as I started, the bell rang again to end recess and I didn't even get a turn.

After school I was doing some math homework when the phone rang. Mom was out in the barn. I picked up the phone and said, "Hello."

"Hello, Natalie." It was him! He'd phoned me!

"It's Mr. Martin," he said.

"Oh, hello," I replied, trying to stay calm and wondering what we would talk about.

"Is your mom home?" he asked.

"My mom? Er, no. I mean yes. But she's out in the barn."

I tried not to sound disappointed. He wanted to talk to Mom, not me. Then my heart really started to pound. Was he going to tell her what I'd said about Dolly Parton or tell her what I'd written in my story when I got the words all mixed up? Or maybe he was going to tell Mom about my other creative writing piece—when he asked us to write and tell how our lives would be different if we'd been born the opposite sex.

I'd written that the only advantage I could see to being a boy was that I'd finally get to see what the inside of a boys' washroom looked like. He'd probably say, "Mrs. Webster, you have a very strange daughter. Have you considered taking her to a psychiatrist?" Or maybe he was going to tell Mom about the other day when I yelled out, "Oh barf," when my pencil broke in the pencil sharpener and the superintendent was visiting our class to check up on Mr. Martin's teaching. Mr. Martin had frowned at me.

"Natalie! Natalie!" I heard his voice.

"Yes?" I said.

"Please ask your mother to give me a call when she comes in. She has my number."

"Yes. OK, I'll tell her," I said faintly and hung up the phone.

When Mom came in, I told her he'd phoned.

"Oh, thanks," Mom said. "It must be about the playground." She called him back right away but I couldn't hear what she said, because our phone is next to the broom closet, and when you want to have a private conversation you only have to step inside and close the door with the phone cord stretched a little bit.

I bit my nails, hoping he wouldn't say anything about the things I'd thought about earlier. But then I figured Mom wouldn't really mind about most of them except maybe me saying "Barf!" when the superintendent was in the room. I could expect a lecture on using unladylike words and being rude.

"Well," Mom said as she stepped out of the closet and hung up the phone, "the model is ready and we can put it on display in the school next week. After that we'll go to the school board to see if they approve and are willing to provide some money. You kids at school can make sugges- tions for changes that are reasonable. Mind—no water slides or anything like that," she went on, almost out of breath.

I thought, This playground really means a lot to her. She's more excited about it than the kids at school.

"Oh, I have a surprise," Mom continued. "We'll be having a visitor for supper on Saturday."

"Not Mr. Martin," I gasped.

"Promise you won't say anything at school."

I promised. I could hardly wait until Saturday. He was coming to visit.

I'd read about girls in Spain or someplace who were not allowed to go out on a date with a man without someone called a chaperone going along to make sure they behaved. They couldn't even hold hands or anything. We would have to make polite conversation and be very proper while Mom acted as our chaperone. Or was I only dreaming?

I asked Mom why he was coming, but she was rather vague. She said something about the playground and then laughingly told me that Mr. Martin wanted to tell her about the things I'd been up to in school. I wasn't absolutely sure she was joking. I had the impression that she hadn't told me everything. Anyway, I was excited about his visit—but a little worried too.

CHAPTER FOUR

Saturday was a warm day, what Mom called Indian summer. He drove into our yard early in the afternoon. He was dressed in jeans and a windbreaker. I'd never seen him in jeans before. I was out on the deck, waiting nervously, sitting on the bench.

"Hi!" I said, as he walked up the steps.

"Hi, Natalie," he smiled.

Mom came out the back door at the same time and called, "Come on in and have a drink. I have to go and give one of the cows a shot. Work on the farm never stops. I won't be long."

"Can I help?" he asked. "I'd like to if you'll let me."

"You'll get your shoes messed up. Wait a minute—there's a pair of rubber boots here somewhere." Mom disappeared into the porch and came out a moment later with a pair of my dad's old rubbers in her hand. "Try these and see if they fit," she said.

Mr. Martin slipped off his shoes and tried on the boots. "They're fine," he said. "A perfect fit."

"Great!" Mom said. "I'll just get the needle. Natalie, you can come and help too, but you'd better put your boots on."

I wrinkled my nose. Chasing a cow around a corral in rubber boots was not my idea of being glamorous.

"And you'd better put on your old jeans," Mom added. "You'll get those good ones messed up."

She went inside and I followed, leaving Mr. Martin standing on the deck. I went to my room. By the time I'd changed and got my rubber boots on, Mom and Mr. Martin were walking down the driveway towards the corral.

The cows were close by in the pasture. Mom lured them into the corral with a bucket of chop, and I closed the gate behind them, locking them in.

"It's the one with the long horns," Mom called to me and Mr. Martin. "She has a touch of foot rot. I have to give her a shot of penicillin. Can you run her into that chute, Mr. Martin? I'll go ahead and adjust the head gate and catch her when she gets to the other end."

Mr. Martin advanced on the cow and waved his arms. Two other cows plus the one with the long horns ran into the chute.

"I'm afraid there are two others ahead of the one you want," he called to Mom.

"That's OK," she said. "If you walk behind them they'll walk around. I'll let the first two out at this end and catch her in the gate when she gets here. Natalie, you close the gate behind Mr. Martin and then come over here and hold the needle for me."

Mr. Martin prodded the long-horned cow forward, forcing the other two to walk ahead and around the chute. I closed the gate behind him and the cows and then climbed over the corral rail to where Mom was waiting. The cows saw me and stopped suddenly. Mr. Martin went right up behind them to get them moving again. Unfortunately he got too close and the long-horned cow did what all cows do when they get nervous. He swore softly, and I saw Mom clap a hand over her mouth to hide a grin. I heard her say, "Oh dear."

I was horrified. Mr. Martin had come here as a guest. I wanted to make a good impression, and the first thing that happens is that one of our cows does a poop in his boot.

Mr. Martin squelched around behind the cows and I helped Mom with the needle when she caught the cow in the gate. "I'm sorry," Mom said to Mr. Martin, as she gave the cow the shot with speed and skill that always amazed me, something she was much better at doing than Dad had been. Mr. Martin and Mom looked at each other, and then they both burst out laughing. I didn't think it was funny at all. I thought it was gross and embarrassing.

After Mom released the cow we went back to the house, and Mom washed Mr. Martin's jeans and sock while he sat around in a pair of my dad's old pants.

I changed into my good jeans again and a new pink blouse. I look good in pink. Mom changed too and put on one of her dresses. It was one I hadn't seen her wear for a long time and she looked really pretty. Mr. Martin commented on it and told her she looked really nice. "You too, Natalie. It's not often I get to dine out with two beautiful ladies."

We had a roast for supper and our own home-grown vegetables. Mr. Martin had brought a bottle of wine, and Mom let me have a small glass. I didn't really like it. It tasted sour but, of course, I didn't say anything.

We talked, or rather Mr. Martin and Mom did, about lots of things, but mostly about school. I was relieved that none of my embarrassments in class were mentioned by Mr. Martin.

Mom told him about the farm, the cattle, "which you've already met," she said—and they both started laughing again. Mom told him about the beehives we had and he seemed really interested. "Natalie is a great help," Mom said. "She helps me when I open the hives, and she isn't afraid of being stung."

"I wear a suit and veil and gloves though," I said. "That helps a lot." Mom told him how we extracted our honey and offered him some with his coffee.

After supper he helped Mom dry the dishes, and I got to watch TV instead of my usual drying job. Actually, I would have been quite willing to have dried the dishes with him and let Mom go and watch TV so that we could have been alone, but Mom knows I hate drying dishes and would be sure to wonder what was going on.

He left just before my bedtime, and Mom and I both saw him to the door. "You get ready for bed," Mom said to me and stepped outside with Mr. Martin.

"Goodbye, Natalie," he called.

"Goodbye," I said. "See you Monday."

When I went to the bathroom to brush my teeth I found we were out of my favourite toothpaste. I stood on the toilet seat to reach the medicine cabinet to look for some more toothpaste, and I happened to look out the window. Mom and Mr. Martin were standing close together beside his car and Mom was holding his hand. What's going on? I thought. Could he be asking Mom for my hand in marriage? From what I'd heard and read in stories, the man has to ask a girl's father for permission to marry his daughter, but since I didn't have a father, maybe Mr. Martin was asking my mother.

I could imagine him saying, "I know she's young, but I'm willing to wait." I'd heard of girls in India, younger than me, being promised in marriage to older men. Then I wondered: if he is asking for my hand, why is he holding Mom's hand?

I couldn't see any more because at that moment I slipped and fell off the toilet seat. By the time I got up again and looked out, he had driven away. I brushed my teeth, my mind in a whirl, and went to bed.

I couldn't sleep. I tossed and turned for quite a while trying to figure out my next move. Somehow I had to let him know how I felt. I had to persuade him to wait at least until I graduated from high school.

If he had been asking Mom for my hand in marriage and she refused, would he wait until I was old enough to say yes myself? If I didn't let him know how I felt, he'd be sure to meet someone else. I'd have to watch out for Ms. Skelly, the gym teacher. She seemed to be coming on really strong when I saw her chatting to him in the gym last week as I was coming out of the girls' changing room. I didn't think Ms. Skelly was his type, but I couldn't be sure. She needed to lose some weight off her hips, and her teeth stuck out.

I must have fallen asleep then. I had this strange dream.

I was sitting in my wedding gown at the front of the class at Mr. Martin's desk. He was sitting beside me, holding my hand. I could smell his aftershave lotion. My dress had a really long train that wound up and down the room between the rows of desks.

The other kids were sitting in their desks. All the boys had their hair slicked down. They had red carnations in the buttonholes of the suits they were wearing. The girls had long, fancy dresses on, and Janet was sitting in her desk holding my flowers.

Kevin Windslow got up out of his desk and stood in front of me and Mr. Martin. We both stood up. Kevin was wearing a pale pink suit with a red carnation like the others, but I noticed he was still wearing his dirty old sneakers. I thought he was going to perform the marriage ceremony and say the proper words, but all he said was, "How ya doin', Nat?"

All of a sudden his red carnation squirted water in my face. Then the fire bell went off. All the kids leaped out of their desks and tramped all over my long dress as they rushed for the door.

I woke up then with the alarm clock ringing madly beside me. I sat up and switched it off. I realized I'd forgotten it was Sunday and I'd set the alarm as usual.

I lay there trying to remember other parts of my dream before it all faded away. I hoped Mr. Martin gave Kevin a detention for squirting me in the face, and I wondered why I was getting married in the classroom.

At breakfast Mom asked me, "Natalie, do you like Mr. Martin?"

"Yeah," I said, "he's neat! I really like him." I couldn't tell her I was in love with him. She already seemed embarrassed, and I wasn't sure what he had said to her last night. He wouldn't really have any idea how I felt about him, and I knew even if he felt the same way about me, he couldn't say anything about it.

The principal, Mr. Stanley, and the school board would have a fit if Mr. Martin announced that we were getting engaged or anything. Mom didn't say any more. Although I was dying to talk about him all I could think of was, "What do you think of him, Mom?"

I saw her blush. "I think he's very nice," she said.

"I wish I was older," I sighed, "at least seventeen."

"Why?" Mom sounded surprised. "You don't want to rush things—you'll be seventeen before you know it. I can't believe how the time has flown since..." She broke off and I knew she was thinking about Dad. She often did that—stopped talking, I mean, when she thought about Dad.

Sometimes I would see tears in her eyes.

She looked at me and smiled. "You'll grow up so fast you'll wish you were ten again. Why do you want to be seventeen so quickly?"

"Well," I said, "Janet says..." I always used Janet when I didn't want to tell my true feelings. That way I wouldn't get blamed if my ideas sounded crazy. I knew Janet did the same thing with her parents—often starting out a conversation when she wanted something with "Natalie says..."

"Janet says what?" Mom prodded.

"Janet says that when you're seventeen you can stay up late and you can have dates and boyfriends and stuff, you're more..." I paused. I couldn't think of the word I wanted.

"Independent?" Mom suggested.

"Yeah, more independent," I said.

"Well, do you feel you're not independent now?" she asked. "I would say you are very independent. I can depend on you to do lots of things. I can trust you. Boys and dates will come soon enough, don't be impatient. What else does Janet have to say?"

I knew she didn't really want to hear what Janet had to say. She knew the game Janet and I played, and she was giving me the chance to say what I thought without me being embarrassed. I knew we were only pretending the ideas were Janet's.

If I really told her what Janet said about teen-agers, Mom would be really embarrassed. Like the time Janet said she hid in her sister's closet when her sister's boyfriend came over and they thought no one else was in the house.

"That's about all," I said.

"Well," Mom smiled and patted my hand, "you can't always believe what Janet says."

I knew she was referring to the time I'd told her I didn't want any more cucumber sandwiches in my lunch. She had been surprised because they had always been my favourite. Then she found out that Janet's father had told her cucumbers put hair on your chest. I had checked my chest in the bathroom mirror for days afterwards.

CHAPTER FIVE

On Monday Mr. Martin announced that he would like all of us to work on a science project of our own, something we were interested in and could tell the class about. We could use anything we liked, and we would demonstrate and display it in class. He said he'd like us to have it ready in two weeks.

Here was another chance for me to make a big impression on Mr. Martin. But what could I do? I wasn't that keen on science, but he'd said it could be anything we were interested in, our own project. Surely I could dream up something really neat in two weeks.

At recess Janet asked, "What are you going to do for the science project?"

"I haven't decided," I said.

"I have. I'm going to have a machine that tells what kind of person you are from your hand-writing."

"How would it work?" I asked.

"I dunno, but it sounds neat and my sister says you can tell what people are like just by the way they write their names. It wouldn't be that hard," she went on. "I'd get all the kids in the class to write their names on pieces of paper and stick the papers in my machine. Then I'd tell them what kind of people they are, one by one. It should be easy to describe those pests Kevin and Billy, and I could say something about every kid in the class."

"But you'd only be making it up," I said. "Mr. Martin wouldn't let you do it as a science project!"

"He might if I had a light bulb that lit up when I shoved the piece of paper with the person's name on it inside the machine. Anyway, it would be a lot more fun than demonstrating how magnets work or something. I started writing out some stuff about some of the kids during math today. Want to hear what I wrote about you?" She pulled a crumpled bit of paper out of her jeans. "Natalie Webster," she read. "Friendly, but sometimes a bit stuck up—daydreams and falls in love a lot."

"What do you mean, 'stuck up'?" I asked.

"Well, you know. Remember that time you had that birthday party and didn't invite me?"

"That was the time you had chicken pox and Mom was afraid I might get it if you came," I retorted.

47

"So, you still didn't invite me."

Sometimes it's no use arguing with Janet. "OK," I said. "What about that other bit, 'falls in love easily'? You can't just make it up."

"Sure I can. Anyway it's true. You're in love with someone now."

"Who?" I asked, blushing.

"I'll never tell," she smirked. "It's a secret, but I know, and if it isn't true, how come your face is all red?"

"Janet, you're crazy and so is your idea." I was glad to hear the bell ring for the end of recess. I was pretty sure Janet really didn't know my secret, she was just making it up.

Janet's idea sounded crazy, all right, but I had to admit it sure sounded interesting. I thought about all sorts of things like cells, stars, and electricity, but none of them appealed to me. I was hopeless with electricity and wouldn't be any good with wires and batteries. All I could think of to do with stars was to draw charts. Cells were pretty small, but I could borrow a microscope at school, I thought. Then I heard that Marie Lacroix had the same idea. No, it had to be something different.

And then I remembered our bees. Actually I saw the movie *The Swarm* on TV. It was all about killer bees. Mom saw it too and said, "That's ridiculous. There are killer bees, but they don't behave anything like the ones in that movie. We don't have them in Canada, thank heavens."

The kids in school were all talking about *The Swarm* the next day. I figured if Janet could enter a science project that was as crazy as her handwriting analysis machine (that's what she called it, but she couldn't spell "analysis"), then I could do something on killer bees and use some of our bees instead. I'd make a big sign with "KILLER BEES" in huge letters on it, and maybe a question mark so I wasn't really saying the bees I had on display were killers. I wasn't even going to use bees that could sting, which were the worker bees. I planned to use drones, which were the male, lazy bees that didn't do anything except mate with the queen. They couldn't sting but they buzzed a lot. They were fat and looked fierce.

I hoped my "KILLER BEES?" sign would get everyone's attention, and then people would read the sheet of information I planned to write about bees. I would include a bit about killer bees, but would go on to explain that the bees they were looking at were actually ordinary honeybee drones. I had to find some way to display them, if I managed to get them in the first place. That was going to be tricky.

A few days later Mr. Martin asked, "How are your science projects coming along? Do you need any help?"

Janet said, "I have mine all planned, but it's

going to be a surprise." She didn't want to get her project cancelled before she unveiled it to the class. She told me she had some really good stuff written up about the "pests," Billy and Kevin. She was making the machine from a shoebox covered in tin foil, and she had a flashlight bulb stuck on top with red cellophane taped to it. The bulb was hooked up to a battery inside the box. It lit up when Janet shoved a piece of paper with someone's name on it into a slot on the box, if she remembered to press a switch underneath.

She demonstrated it to me when I stayed at her house on the weekend. She'd figured out a way to get the machine to feed out the information by writing it on a cash register roll. She put the roll on a roller inside the box and stuck a handle through the side so that the roll with the information on it came out when she turned the handle. I pointed out that she'd have to make sure she put the kids' names in the box in the same order as the stuff she'd written about them on the roll, or it wouldn't work, but she said she'd already thought of that.

Janet asked, "What about your idea? You haven't said anything about yours. You've only got another week."

"I haven't really decided," I lied. I wanted it to be a complete surprise.

"Well, let's try to decide now," she said. "Something really exciting. How about a machine that makes candy or bubble gum. Or how about one that tells who you're going to fall in love with?"

"How?" I said. "They sound crazier than your handwriting analysis machine."

"So?" said Janet. She always said "So?" when she didn't have a good answer. "You know what Jimmy Chan invented?" she asked.

"No, what?" I said.

"He invented a periscope and brought it to school this morning before you got there, and Kevin Windslow grabbed it off him and tried to look up my dress with it."

"What did you do?" I asked.

"He was lying on the floor, and I stepped on him in a place that really hurt," she laughed. "He was still rolling around on the floor when Mr. Martin came in. So what are you going to do?" she asked again.

"I'll think of something," I said. "Did you read any more of your sister's diary?" I asked, to change the subject.

"No," Janet snorted. "She caught me reading it and we had a big fight and she told Mom. Mom said I shouldn't have done that, diaries are private. You can say that again! Some of the stuff she had written was real juicy, but I bet she just made it up. Maybe I could put some of that stuff in my handwriting analysis machine."

"I don't think Mr. Martin would like it," I said.

"Well, it would liven up science. It's so boring," she giggled.

With only three days left before the science projects were due, I found the container I needed to display my bees. It was another small fish tank that wasn't being used and it sat on top of the cupboard in our classroom. I asked Mr. Martin if I could borrow it on science project day.

"Sure, as long as you promise not to put any more guppies in my coffee," he said, laughing.

I didn't tell him what I wanted it for, and he must have thought I was going to bring fish. I planned to bring the bees to school in a shoebox and put them in the tank, with a lid on it, of course. I couldn't get them until just before the science projects were due. I knew that a lot of the bees would die if I kept them in a box with no food.

On the day before science project day, as soon as I got home, I put my lunch kit in the porch and hollered, "Hi, Mom! I'm home and I'm going outside."

"OK," I heard her holler back, and I think she said something else, but I didn't hear what it was because I went outside right away. I wanted to get the drones all by myself so that it was a one-hundred-percent Natalie Webster science project.

I hurried to the honey house—a small shed near the barn where we kept our bee suits and bee-keeping equipment. I'd put the shoebox there earlier in the week. I had taped the lid down and punched a hole in the side and stuffed it with a cork. I had a pair of tweezers to pick up the drones, and I planned to stuff them one by one into the box through the hole and keep them in with the cork. It was going to be tricky.

I changed into my bee suit and made sure my hat and veil were on properly. I slipped on the long gloves. I tucked the pants of my suit into my rubber boots to keep the bees from stinging me on the ankles. I decided to take the smoker but wasn't sure how I would manage to smoke the bees, hold the frames, and pick off the drones at the same time.

I went out to the beehives. I got the smoker going after a few tries. The smoker is a kind of tin can with a spout. You burn a piece of sack in it to make smoke and puff the smoke at the bees by squeezing a little bellows on the side of the can. The smoke is supposed to calm down the bees and keep them from flying at you when you open the hive.

I got the smoker going well, gave it a few good puffs, and got a lot of smoke. I puffed it once in front of the entrance to one of the hives, then I quietly lifted the lid off.

A hive is made up of boxes called supers. The honey supers, where bees store their honey, are always stacked on top of the brood supers, where the queen, her eggs, and the young bees are. I was glad we had taken off all the honey supers earlier, because now the drones were below in the brood supers. I would never have been able to lift a honey super off by myself. They were too heavy.

I took the hive tool from my pocket and eased up the cover of the brood super. I puffed in a little smoke and waited a few seconds. I hoped the bees were in a good mood. Even though I was all covered up, it still made me nervous when bees flew at my face and buzzed angrily outside my veil.

I eased off the cover and put it down beside the hive. The bees seemed to be calm, and only one or two flew around me. There are several frames inside each super. I wanted one from near the centre, where there were lots of bees, including the drones I wanted. I put down the smoker and pried one of the outside frames out with the hive tool. I put it down near my feet and moved some of the other frames over until I could get at a centre frame. I eased it out, being careful not to crush the queen. The bees stayed on the frame and were quiet. They completely covered the frame on both sides. I had to put it down to have my hands free to get the drones. I propped it up against the outside frame I had taken out before.

I saw several drones and began to pick them off one by one with the tweezers, stuffing them into the box and making sure the cork was in place each time. It was slow work, but I got better and faster as I went along. I didn't squash too many, but the drones buzzed loudly when I grabbed them with the tweezers and a few of the workers seemed to get a little angry. I put the frame back and took out another, as I was running short of drones. I gave the hive another puff of smoke. I held my breath when the frame almost slipped from my hand, but most of the bees remained quiet. I worked fast and when I had what I thought were about fifty drones, I put the frames back, replaced the cover and lid, and gathered up my box, smoker, and hive tool. Although it was a cool day, I was sweating under my suit.

I changed quickly, then hurried to the house and put my box of drones in the porch. I planned to put them in my bedroom later to keep them warm, but I didn't want Mom to ask what was in the box. When I went into the kitchen she was all dressed up. She was wearing her pretty flowered dress.

"Oh, there you are. I've been calling you for ages. Where were you?"

"Just outside," I said.

"Are you sure you're OK?" Mom asked. "You look hot."

"Yes, I'm fine," I said.

"I have to go and do a presentation of our playground project to the school board. I'll be late if I don't leave right away. And I'll be late getting home for supper. There's some chicken in the fridge. Heat it up in the microwave and put on some peas or broccoli, and I'll have some later. I'll be back as soon as I can. OK?" She grabbed her purse and the boxes containing the model of the playground off the couch. She went out into the porch, and I went to the fridge to get out the chicken.

I heard the car drive away and I put three pieces of chicken on a plate. I was hungry after my work with the bees. I began to look in the freezer for some frozen peas. I took out a package, and the cold reminded me that the porch isn't all that warm. I decided to move the drones into my bedroom.

I went out to the porch and picked up the shoebox. It seemed heavy. I shook it and instead of making a buzzing sound, it rattled. I lifted the lid and stared in horror at pieces of climber and slide models made from popsicle sticks. "Oh no," I groaned. "Mom has my bees. She must have put her boxes down on the shelf for a minute and picked up mine by mistake." I ran back into the kitchen to try to phone her. I looked up the school district office number and dialled frantically. I listened to the phone ringing but no one answered. I glanced at the clock over the stove and saw it was just after five o'clock. The staff must have gone to the meeting in the council chambers next door, where they couldn't hear the phone.

Oh, what can I do? I thought. I'd never get to town fast enough on my bike—all those hills. Then, without another thought, I grabbed the tractor key off the key rack, threw on my jacket, picked up the box of playground stuff, and raced out to the machine shed.

I climbed up to the high seat of our old John Deere tractor. I'd driven it a couple of times at slow speed in a field, pulling a disc when Mom was getting the field ready to seed. I wasn't too sure about steering it on the road.

I put the shoebox between my feet. I felt scared as I put the key in the ignition. The tractor seemed huge. I put the gear lever into neutral and stepped on the clutch at the same time. I had to almost stand to reach it. I turned the key in the ignition to start the engine. It made a whirring noise and coughed a bit, but it didn't start. The choke! I forgot the choke. I pulled out the choke button and tried again. The motor whirred again and coughed, and this time a puff of black smoke came out of the exhaust pipe, but it still didn't start.

"Oh, come on, come on," I begged. "Start. Start!" Mom called the tractor Old Faithful because she always got it to start easily. I prayed the tractor would live up to its name now. I tried again and opened the throttle a bit more. Maybe it needed more gas. The motor whirred, coughed. More smoke puffed out of the exhaust pipe and there was a loud bang. I jumped and nearly fell off the seat, but the motor caught and I eased the tractor into reverse to back it out of the shed. "Don't stall, please don't stall," I prayed. I slowly reversed the tractor into the yard. I swung the steering wheel and changed into first gear, using the numbers on the gear shift to help me. I eased my foot off the clutch again and the tractor jerked forward down the driveway, towards the road.

I reached the end of the driveway and stopped to make sure nothing was coming. I swung the tractor onto the gravel road towards town. I was still in first gear, but I was going as fast as I'd ever driven it before. I knew I'd have to go faster. I pushed in the choke and the motor quietened down a bit, and I eased the tractor into second gear. I seemed to be flying along, but I knew it would still take ages to get to town. I shifted to third, and the speed really picked up. Power poles went flashing by as Old Faithful charged along. I prayed I wouldn't meet much traffic.

I reached the paved road, which was wider, and again checked for traffic. I waited for a large truck to go by and let the tractor go ahead in first gear, quickly changing to second, then third gear. I was getting the feel of it now and I concentrated on keeping the tractor on the right side of the road. I bit my lip and shifted into fourth gear and opened the throttle. "OK!" I let out a sigh of relief. I should make it now. But would I make it in time?

I reached the outskirts of town and slowed the tractor down, changing into a lower gear. I just couldn't have an accident now. I was nearly there. I headed down the main street. I nearly panicked when a truck came up fast behind me, really close, and then shot past me. I saw the school district offices ahead on the other side of the road. I slowed down, looked quickly behind me, then ahead. I swung the tractor across the street. I was headed straight for the building. I jammed the brakes on but I didn't do it quickly enough. I bit my lip as the tractor stopped with its two front wheels up on the sidewalk. I switched off the motor and jumped down. My legs were trembling, but I grabbed the shoebox and raced for the door.

CHAPTER SIX

I ran into the lobby and saw the door marked "Council Chambers." I pushed open the door and saw Mom standing and talking to the school board members. Mr. Martin was sitting beside her and assembling the model of the playground on the table. I yelled, "Mom! Mom!" Mom stopped speaking and looked up, startled. At the same time Mr. Martin lifted the lid from my box of drones and they poured out, buzzing loudly.

Immediately everyone went crazy. It was just like a scene from *The Swarm*, and the way people acted I'm sure they'd all seen the movie.

Mrs. Bompas started screaming. Mr. Cranshaw, the chairman of the board, banged his gavel, squashing a couple of drones at the same time, although he didn't notice them. I yelled, "They won't sting!" but no one could hear me. Mr. Wentworth headed for the door, shouting, "I'm allergic to bees! Let me out of here!" Mrs. Appleby and Mr. Gordon jumped to their feet and looked unsure of what was happening. Mom and Mr. Martin stared in horror.

The drones, confused and bumbling as usual, flew around, buzzing loudly, crashing into walls and people. Mrs. Bompas's screams rose even higher when Mr. Gordon swatted at one of the drones and accidentally directed it into the top of Mrs. Bompas's low-cut blouse, where it buzzed between her Dolly Partons. Mrs. Bompas always wore low-cut blouses and short skirts, and Mom said she looked ridiculous because she was too chubby. She looked even more ridiculous now as she flapped frantically at her chest. Mr. Gordon got a slap on the face when he tried to help get the drone out. Mr. Cranshaw went on banging his gavel and yelling "Order! Order!" as if he couldn't believe the bees wouldn't obey the chairman.

All this time I had been yelling too. "They're only drones, they're only drones!" Mrs. Appleby decided Mr. Wentworth had the right idea, and everyone followed her out the door except Mom, Mr. Martin and Mr. Cranshaw, who was still trying to conduct a meeting.

I could see Mom was upset. Mr. Gordon ran back in with a can of bug-killer he'd found somewhere and started spraying the room frantically. The room became so filled with fumes that Mr. Cranshaw started choking. Mom took him by the arm and led him outside, giving me a look that said, "Why? How could you do this to me? You'd better have a darn good explanation." Mr. Martin gathered up the playground model pieces as the drones gave their last buzzes under Mr. Gordon's attack and fell to the floor. I stood there, stunned at the mess I'd caused, until Mr. Martin took me by the arm and led me outside.

We were just in time to see Mom, furious and embarrassed, jump onto the seat of Old Faithful and drive off up the street. Obviously she did not want to leave it outside the school district offices where I had caused such a disaster. She sure looked strange, driving a tractor all dressed up. I knew she was really mad because she had jumped onto the tractor and taken off. Mr. Martin and I stood on the sidewalk, and before Mom turned the corner on Old Faithful she looked back once.

Mr. Martin said, "Come on, I'll drive you home." He put me in his car and then went back to the building for a few minutes. I saw him standing on the steps talking to Mr. Cranshaw and Mr. Gordon. Mrs. Bompas and Mr. Wentworth walked past the car a minute later, and I ducked my head so they wouldn't see me. Mrs. Bompas looked shaken as she jiggled past, still patting her neck and chest with a handkerchief, and Mr. Wentworth's hair stood out all over the place where he'd run his hands through it searching for bees.

Mr. Martin came back and got into the car and

started it. "OK," he said, "you'd better tell me what happened."

"I'm sorry," I said. "I didn't plan this." I knew there were tears in my eyes. "I'm sorry I messed things up, but I tried to warn her. It was my science project."

"What?" he said. "You wanted to see how a room full of people would react when you released a box full of bees among them?" He chuckled and patted my arm.

That's one of the things I really like about Mr. Martin, his sense of humour. I looked at him and smiled. He stopped the car and took a white handkerchief from his breast pocket and handed it to me. "Here," he said. I dabbed at my eyes. "Go on, tell me all about it."

"I was going to display the bees in that aquarium in our classroom for my science project tomorrow. They were only drones. They couldn't sting. All the kids have seen *The Swarm* on TV and are interested in bees, and I have my write-up all done. Mom picked up my box of drones instead of this one." I had the box of playground models resting on my knees. "Do you think the playground will be cancelled?" I asked. "Mom will kill me if it is, and so will the kids at school."

"I think I can explain everything, although it may take a while for Mrs. Bompas and Mr. Wentworth to calm down." He restarted the car and started to laugh.

We were halfway home when ahead of us I saw Mom riding high on Old Faithful. I knew she was still mad at me. She was driving fast, something she did when she was mad. Even Old Faithful seemed mad, the way the dust shot up from its wheels.

Mr. Martin pulled out and passed Mom. I didn't dare look back. When we were well ahead he pulled the car over to the side of the road and switched off the motor. He patted my hand and said, "I'll talk to your mom. You stay here." He got out of the car and walked back to meet her.

I sat there with my fingers crossed. "Please, oh please, make everything OK," I prayed. "I've really messed things up this time. Mom's mad at me. I've embarrassed her and maybe ruined any chance of getting the playground built. Mr. Martin will think I'm such a ninny. It was a dumb idea getting the drones." I glanced in the rear-view mirror and saw him standing on the road beside the tractor, looking up at Mom and holding her hand.

I looked away and sighed. I wished he'd hold my hand like he was holding Mom's. He was probably just trying to calm her down. I hoped he was persuading Mom it wasn't my fault.

I heard him open the car door and get in. I looked at him as he started the car. "It's going to be OK," he said. "I've told your mom what happened."

"Thanks," I said, and I never felt so in love with him as I did at that moment. I felt tears in my eyes again and he patted my hand as he drove on.

When we got home I went to the bathroom to wash my face and to give him a chance to talk to Mom some more. He said he'd wait for her outside and I should go in. I looked at my eyes in the mirror. They didn't look too red, but my hair was a bit wild from the tractor ride. I combed it and went to my room and lay down on my bed. I still wasn't really ready to face Mom.

I vowed to make it up to her, and I'd have to show Mr. Martin how I felt about him too. He'd said my science project was a good idea and it wasn't my fault.

I must have dozed off then, because the next thing I knew Mom was tapping on my door. She stuck her head in and smiled at me. "Ready for some supper?" She came in and hugged me. "It's OK. Eric told me everything. It was my fault. I was in such a rush. I'm sorry I ruined your science project." I hugged her.

"I was more upset," she went on, "when I realized you had driven that old tractor all the way into town. You could have been killed. I know why you did it now. When I came out of the building after what had happened with the bees, I just wanted to get away from there. I just didn't think, and when I saw Old Faithful I was even more upset. I couldn't bear to leave the tractor parked outside as a reminder of what had happened. I had to get it away from there, so I just jumped onto it and drove off—I was very angry with you. I'm sorry. I saw you with Eric before I turned the corner, and I knew somehow he would drive you home." We hugged each other and both of us cried a little.

I was happy. Eric—she'd called him Eric. She usually referred to him as Mr. Martin. "Why did you call him Eric?" I asked.

"Well, he's a pretty good friend to both of us."

"Does he call you Jennifer?" I asked.

"Sometimes," Mom said, and wiped a tear from her eye. "Now let's have supper."

We had the chicken and said nothing more about what had happened. After supper the phone rang and Mom answered it. I heard her say, "Oh dear," then, "Thanks again for everything. I really appreciate it."

"That was Mr. Martin," Mom said. "He's explained everything to Mr. Cranshaw who, it seems, has a sense of humour. He's not so sure about Mrs. Bompas and Mr. Wentworth, especially Mrs. Bompas. She'd wanted to use the playground money to pay for repainting the high school gym, and Mr. Cranshaw feels he will have to do a lot of talking now to persuade her. Oh well," Mom smiled, "not to worry—we'll get it built somehow. By the way, Eric said we probably won't have to make another presentation about the playground to the school board—that's a relief anyway.''

I squeezed her hand and went and got ready for bed, hoping that things would turn out OK.

That night I had another crazy dream in which Mr. Cranshaw kept squashing drones with his gavel as I passed them to him one by one, and Mrs. Bompas, wearing a beekeeper's hat and veil, was marrying Mr. Martin.

CHAPTER SEVEN

Next day in school all the kids, except me, unveiled their science projects. Janet asked me as soon as I got there, "Where's your science project?"

"It didn't work out," I said. "I just brought the write-up." I had my poster and write-up about killer bees and regular bees rolled up under my arm.

Mr. Martin said we could spend the whole morning showing and explaining our science projects to the rest of the class. He looked at me and smiled. "Now who's going to go first?" Nobody wanted to be first so he said he'd pick someone. The first one he picked was Jimmy Chan. He showed off his periscope and explained how it worked. I heard Janet snort and mutter about Kevin using it to look up girls' dresses.

After Jimmy, lots of kids volunteered. Mr. Martin put a list of the names of the kids who raised their hands on the board and they took turns explaining their experiments and gadgets.

Tony Jackson demonstrated his electric tester, which was a card with pictures of birds on it, with the names of the birds mixed up. When you touched a wire to a bird and another to the right name, a little bulb lit up. Mr. Martin thought it was pretty neat and so did I, but then I remembered Tony Jackson's father is an electrician and probably had helped him.

Kathy Kuryluk had a small volcano made of papier-mache, which poured out smoke and other stuff that was supposed to be lava when you lit some chemicals in it with a match. It got pretty smoky in the room and Mr. Martin had to open a window.

Paul Schwitzer had a gerbil that was supposed to run around in a wheel and generate electricity, and light up a bulb. But it was too frightened by all the smoke from Kathy's volcano and by all the kids staring at it, so it wouldn't run in the wheel.

After recess it was my turn, and I showed my poster about killer bees and mentioned *The Swarm*. Mr. Martin sat at the back of the class. I saw him smile a couple of times and I guessed he was thinking of what had happened the day before. No one knew, except Mr. Martin, that I had intended to show them some real bees. The kids were interested in what I told them about ordinary honey bees as well as killer bees and asked me some questions. They really liked the samples of comb honey Mom had wrapped up for me that morning. Mr. Martin said it was a good presentation when I had finished.

The highlight of the day, however, was Janet's handwriting analysis machine. She had a sign on a piece of cardboard and I noticed she still had "analysis" spelled wrong. She'd found a book about handwriting in the public library and had one or two ideas from it on her sign. The rest, of course, she had made up. She explained that she needed a sample of everyone's writing. All the kids volunteered to write their names out right away. Then Janet explained that her machine would tell what their characters were like and might even tell their futures.

She handed out bits of paper and we all wrote our names. She collected them and took a minute or two to sort them. The rest of the kids didn't know it, but I knew she was putting their names in the same order as the stuff she had written on the roll.

When she was ready she read out the first name and stuffed the slip of paper into a slot in the box. She flicked the switch. The red light bulb came on and she turned the handle on the side to crank out the kid's analysis.

The first one was Steven Bradshaw, the class brain. Janet read, "This person is very smart and gets high marks in all subjects. He will probably be a brain surgeon or a scientist."

Everything went well, but Mr. Martin looked a bit worried and had a whispered conversation with Janet when he'd heard one or two readings that seemed a little rude, like the one for Betsy Bridges: she would have fifteen children and two affairs (Janet loved the word "affair" and used it in a few readings). She assured Mr. Martin that no one would mind and he let her continue when the class showed they weren't upset but loved it and wanted to hear more.

Paul LeMay was described as "kind to animals, a good student, friendly, with great muscles." Janet liked him and wanted him to like her.

About Tony Jackson she said, "This person is a bit of a show-off but only sometimes. He loves bubble gum and shouldn't bug other kids." Once she tore too much paper off the end of the roll and had to stick her finger inside the box to find the end again to read out Michelle Carson's. She got it going again.

"Billy Pinchback—well, what does the hand-writing analysis machine say about him?" We all waited expectantly. Janet let us wait, enjoying the hush and the suspense. Everyone knew how she felt about Billy. He grinned from ear to ear, enjoying his role as class pest, along with Kevin Windslow, who grinned back at him. "This person," Janet read, "will soon be one of the best students in school, working hard to improve his marks in all subjects. He won't bother other kids, especially girls, from now on. He is going to change. Because," Janet added, "if he doesn't, I will tell a big secret about him that is written here." Billy continued to grin but I saw a worried look cross his face for a minute. I guess he was wondering if Janet really did know some secret about him.

When she came to my name she read, "This person wants to be a vet—she will marry the man of her dreams." The class tittered and I blushed. For a moment I thought Janet knew more than I thought she knew and would actually name Mr. Martin as my future husband. I was relieved when she went on to the next person.

It was supposed to be Kevin Windslow but Alex Klemchuk was absent. Because Janet hadn't allowed for anyone being absent she read Alex's analysis out for Kevin. Everything she said was pretty nice, and after she read it she looked puzzled. So did the rest of the class, including Kevin, who thought Janet was up to some trick. She realized her mistake and was about to read out the right one for Kevin when Mr. Martin said, "That's fine, Janet. Thanks, but I think we'd better give the others a chance to tell about their projects before we run out of time."

It was lucky she didn't read out the real piece she'd written for Kevin, because she told me later that she'd described him as a future sex maniac who would go to prison for life, or at least get the electric chair.

A few days later news of the disaster with the bees leaked out. It appeared in the local newspaper, *The Elmwood Bugle*, with the headline, "Board Buzzes with Excitement." I hadn't realized one of the people sitting in the council chambers was a reporter. Luckily, my part in the disaster wasn't mentioned, because the reporter had run for his life and rushed outside like everyone else when the bees escaped. He wasn't sure where the bees had come from. The paper said, "The bees suddenly appeared while Mrs. J. Webster was making a presentation on behalf of the Parent-Teacher Committee of Elmwood Elementary about an adventure playground for the school." The paper went on, "Maybe it would be a good thing to happen more often at meetings to prevent people from droning on and on." Mom told me that was a pun.

Janet's mother, of course, heard about it from Mom, and I had to tell Janet all about it. She laughed her head off when I told her about Mrs. Bompas. Her respect for Mr. Martin rose a few notches too when I told her how he had explained everything to Mom.

"Your mom's pretty nice too," she said. "My mom would kill me if I did something like that, even if it wasn't my fault."

Although my name hadn't been mentioned, all

the kids knew that the Mrs. J. Webster in the paper was my mom. Some kids made a few comments and for a few days I would hear one or two making buzzing noises when they glanced at me. Janet is a real friend sometimes—she silenced them with one of her hard stares that meant, "Shut up or it'll be worse for you."

CHAPTER EIGHT

I decided to write a love poem. A love note wasn't good enough. It had to be a poem, a sort of valentine to tell him how I felt about him. Not the kind of valentine that kids give to each other on Valentine's Day, or the kind they give their teacher, like "You're a whale of a teacher," with a cartoon of a whale on it. This was serious. I had to make him understand how I felt. I couldn't just walk up to him and say "Mr. Martin," or "Eric, I love you. Will you wait for me and marry me when I'm old enough?" Anyway, I still thought it should be the man who asks the girl, although on TV I'd seen a girl ask a man. What I wanted to do was to give him some sign.

Janet is a great believer in signs and good luck charms. She often wears a rabbit's foot on a chain around her neck for good luck, especially when we're going to have a test in school. She says sometimes you have to make things happen and give the good luck charm a bit of help, like writing a few answers on the back of your hand before the test.

Well, I was going to make things happen too. I couldn't go on like this much longer. I knew that because of his age and his job Mr. Martin couldn't give me a sign about how he felt. It was up to me. So I decided to write him a love poem.

I spent ages looking through poetry books in the school library and in a few we had at home to get some ideas, but I couldn't find anything I liked. It had to be in my own words, but I wanted it to be good.

I found two old records of Mom's at home, one by a singer named Doris Day called "Secret Love" and another by Paul Anka that began, "I'm So Young and You're So Old." I played them over and over because they sort of said what I wanted to say, but I still wanted to use my own words. "Secret Love" was my favourite. It was awful having to keep my feelings a secret. If only I knew how he felt about me. If only I knew he felt the same and would wait until I graduated, then everything would be fine. It would be our secret. As long as I knew he'd wait for me, I'd be happy.

I sat down to try to write my poem lots of times, but nothing would come right. I'd start with phrases like "My love for you will never die," but then I would get my ideas and words mixed up with the words of "Secret Love" and

"I'm So Young and You're So Old." I even thought of starting the poem out with that line, but I thought Mr. Martin would be insulted. Adults don't like to be told they are old. Besides, if my mom knew that song he probably did too, and he'd know I hadn't made it up myself.

Once or twice Mom found me in my room chewing on a pencil with a few scribblings on some paper in front of me. "Doing some homework?" she asked once.

"Mmm, yeah, sort of," I said.

"Need any help?" she asked.

"No, no," I replied hurriedly. "It's just a story I'm working on, it's not really homework. I'm just doodling."

I decided to stop trying to write when Mom was around. It was making me nervous. I decided to wait until I went to bed. Sometimes I would sit up and read for a while in bed before I went to sleep. I'd write my poem then.

Still nothing worked. I crumpled up piece of paper after piece of paper and hid them in my drawer until I could burn them in our fireplace. I didn't want to leave any evidence around for Mom to find. It would be a shock for her and, although she is very kind and understanding, it wasn't something I could talk over with her. I didn't think she would understand my feelings for Mr. Martin. I didn't understand them myself. I only knew I had them.

In the next two weeks I struggled with my poem, never satisfied with my efforts. I fell asleep once with the light on and a pencil in my hand and woke with a start when Mom switched off my light. I sat up in bed and switched on the light again. My piece of paper with the words I'd written was still under my hand. Mom hadn't noticed it. I read it again.

"Although I'm only eleven today," I lied (I still had three months to go before I'd be eleven), "I'm writing this to you to say, I love you." "Oh barf," I said. "It sounds like one of those sick valentine cards." I crumpled up the paper and tossed it into my drawer and switched off the light again.

I guess I fell asleep then and I must have dreamed, because when I woke up and switched on the light it was three in the morning and words for my poem were running through my head. I grabbed my pencil and a new piece of paper. I was inspired. It took only a few minutes but I'd written my poem. It felt right too. I had scribbled it out quickly, but I would write it out in my best handwriting tomorrow.

I fell asleep happy.

I planned to slip the poem into his lesson plan book on his desk at home time. I didn't want him to find it with the whole class in the room and have him ask me about it. I wanted him to read it alone without interruption. It was meant to be read in private, not with twenty-four kids sitting around talking and throwing spitballs.

I had put the poem in an envelope and even sprinkled a few drops of one of Mom's perfumes inside the envelope before I sealed it. The perfume was called First Love, which I thought was the perfect name.

For three days I carried the poem back and forth to school in my lunch kit, never getting the right opportunity to slip it into his plan book.

I began to get worried that the perfume would wear off and my poem would begin to smell like a tuna fish sandwich. I couldn't bring myself to hand it to him. I wanted him to find it when I wasn't there, although I was dying to see his reaction when he read it.

Whenever the home bell rang he was either sitting at his desk, reading to us, or standing by the blackboard, teaching about stars or something. He'd tell us bus kids to put away our books and get our things and line up. We were always the first kids to leave. Each time I had to slip the envelope back into my lunch kit and line up with the bus kids until the final bell rang.

It wasn't until Friday that I got my chance. Just before home time we were doing some spelling in our scribblers. "Can I have your attention?" he said. "I want to remind you about the poem I asked you to learn for Monday."

Kathy Kuryluk raised her hand. "I left my

poem in the pocket of my jeans and my mom threw them in the wash."

"You were supposed to glue the poem into your poetry scribbler," Mr. Martin said. "I'll get you another copy."

He got up and left the room with a copy of the poem in his hand and headed for the workroom.

The bell rang almost immediately and the kids started picking up and putting away their books. Several left their desks to put things in their lunch kits and put away textbooks. There was quite a bit of noise and confusion, so I seized my chance.

I slipped the envelope with my poem inside my spelling text and headed towards the shelf where the spelling texts were stored. I took the long way round, past Mr. Martin's desk. When I reached it, I slowed down, turned my back on the class, and slipped the poem out of my speller and inside his open lesson plan book. I closed his book and continued on towards the shelf. One or two other kids were putting their spelling texts away too. I looked around to see if anyone had noticed, but most of the kids were watching Michael Collins and Jason Hopkins scuffling over something.

Just then Mr. Martin came back and nearly everyone dived for the desks. As I put my spelling text on the pile on the shelf, I hoped I looked as cool as a cucumber, even though my heart was pounding like mad.

"Here's your poem, Kathy," Mr. Martin said. "Try not to lose it this time. OK, everyone. Don't leave any lunch bags or kits on the shelf when you leave. Bus students, it's time to go."

CHAPTER NINE

Janet was going to spend the weekend so she came home with me on the school bus. She brought along her favourite doll, and it was all she seemed to talk about on the way home.

"Natalie, you're not listening to me." She dug me in the ribs with her elbow.

"Oh yeah. Sorry, Janet. I guess I don't really feel like playing with dolls."

"What's got into you lately? Don't you want to play? I can't go home now—my mom would give me heck if I phoned her and told her I wanted to go home. She and Dad are having a big date tonight, and my sister and brother are going to be away too. Mom and Dad want to be alone, if you know what I mean."

"Yeah," I said again. I didn't feel like playing with dolls. I had suddenly become too grown-up for that sort of thing. It was too babyish for someone in love.

The bus eased to a stop at my driveway and we hopped off. "See you Monday," called Mrs. Sparks, our bus driver.

As we walked down the driveway, Janet asked, "Well, what will we do first?"

"Let's have a snack," I said. "I'm hungry. Mom promised to bake some cookies."

"Sounds great," said Janet. "Race you." We dashed down the driveway towards the house.

"Hi, Natalie. How are you, Janet?" Mom asked us as we went into the kitchen.

"Pretty good," Janet said.

"You can put your bag in Natalie's room," Mom said. "You know where it is." We hung up our coats and Janet went to my room.

"Any lemonade?" I asked.

"Yes, there's a new container in the fridge," Mom said. "Help yourself." I went and got it as Janet came back.

"Want some lemonade?"

"Yeah, sure thing."

We sat down at the kitchen table and I poured the lemonade. Mom brought a plate of her home-made cookies and sat down with us.

"Mmm, these are good," Janet said.

"How was school today?" Mom asked.

"Pretty good," I said.

"OK, I guess," Janet mumbled, her mouth full of cookie. "But I hate the way the Grade 7s act. They walk down the hall laughing at us because they're bigger. They get to stay in at recess, and we get booted out or get a D.T. They think they own the world."

Mom laughed. "I'm sure they aren't supposed to be in at recess, they're probably just harder to get out."

"Yeah," Janet said. "They're sneaky."

"Well," Mom said, "it won't be long before both of you are in Grade 7 and you'll feel like you own the world too. By the way, I hadn't planned this, but I've been invited out to supper tonight and I've asked Mrs. Stevenson to look in on you around eight-thirty to make sure everything is OK. Your supper will be ready in about an hour. I'll get it all ready, and you'll only have to serve yourselves. I shouldn't be very late. I checked with your mom, Janet, and she said it's fine. She and I think both of you are old enough to be left alone for a little while now. You're not Grade 7s, I know, but I think you're responsible. I'll leave the phone number where I'll be in case you need to get in touch with me."

"Can we make some popcorn tonight?" I asked. "Sure," Mom said.

We finished our lemonade. "Well, I'd better start getting ready," Mom said. "I've already taken care of the chickens, so you and Janet can go and play until supper is ready. If you go outside, don't go too far away, though. I'm going to cook you a pepperoni pizza. I'll get it ready just before I leave. It only takes about fifteen minutes in the oven and I'll turn it off before I go. I'll ring the bell when I'm ready to leave and you can come in and eat."

"I love pepperoni pizza," Janet said.

"What do you want to do?" I asked her.

"Let's go outside and play for a while, then I want you to hear my new Bruce Springsteen record after supper. I brought it with me. It's really great."

We put on our coats and went outside. Although it was the middle of November, it was still pretty nice out.

"Let's go and look at the cows," Janet said. "Maybe your bull will be doing something this time." She was always hoping to see our bull "doing something," as she put it, but so far she had been disappointed on all her visits to our farm. We climbed through the barbed-wire fence into the pasture. The cattle were on the other side of the field near some trees.

As we walked towards them Janet asked, "What do you think of Paul LeMay?"

"I think he's cute," I said.

"Yeah, what muscles! But I think he's got a girlfriend. It's no use wasting time looking at cute boys with girlfriends." She went on, "Do you know what I dreamed last night?"

"No, what?"

"I dreamed I got married to Mr. T."

"Him?" I said. "Do you know how old he is? How can you stand his voice?"

"He's at least forty-three, and I can't help it—it was only a dream anyway. If I was married to him I'd have an affair."

"Was that in your dream too?" I asked.

"No, but I would."

We reached the cattle and patted one of the tamer calves. Most of them wouldn't come near us, but this one was friendly. Mom and I had to start feeding him with a bottle when he was born because he was weak.

"Where's the bull?" Janet asked.

"Over there," I pointed. "He's lying down under that tree."

"Gosh, he's lazy. Doesn't he ever do anything? I don't understand how these calves ever get born. If I was one of these cows I'd have an affair."

"That would be pretty hard to do," I giggled. "There's only one bull."

"Well, I wouldn't stick around. I'd jump the fence and look for another bull or something. If I was one of these cows, I'd get a divorce. Your bull is so boring," Janet scoffed. "Come on, let's play in your treehouse."

We crossed the field again, went back through the fence, and climbed the ladder to the small treehouse at the edge of the lawn. My dad had built it for me, but I didn't use it much now unless Janet or one of my other friends came for a visit.

Janet especially liked it, because she thought it was a really private place. She wished she had a place where she could escape from what she called her bratty brother and sister.

The treehouse had a roof and it was nice and dry inside. It had a small window at one end, and you had to duck your head to get inside the door. When we stood inside, our heads almost touched the ceiling.

"Hey," I said, "I must have grown some more. My head's just about to the ceiling." We sat on the piece of carpeting that I'd dragged inside when Mom had recarpeted the living room and I got to keep a piece of the old stuff.

"What do you want to talk about?" Janet asked. She always wanted to talk about something private or secret when we sat in the treehouse because she knew we couldn't be overheard. Usually we talked about boys.

"I don't know," I said. I was silent for a few minutes.

Janet looked at me. "What are you thinking about?"

Could I trust her? I wondered. She *is* my best friend. I was bursting to tell someone, but would I be able to make her understand?

"Natalie, I'm talking to you. Are you deaf?" she asked loudly.

"Uh-huh. I mean no. You know that dream you said you had about marrying Mr. T?"

"Yeah," Janet said. "It was really funny."

"What do you think it would be like to marry an older man?" I asked.

"I dunno. It depends on how old, if he was rich or not. I wouldn't want to marry an old guy if he was poor. It would be neat to be so rich you could have servants. I wouldn't have to do things like cleaning off the table and stuff."

"Yeah," I said. "I had a dream."

"Tell me about it." She looked at me expectantly.

"Promise you won't laugh," I said. "Promise."

"But what if it's really funny?" Janet asked. "How can I promise not to laugh if it's really funny? Some dreams are hilarious."

"Then I won't tell you. Anyway it's serious. It isn't funny," I said.

"OK. Tell me. I promise I won't laugh."

"You've got to promise not to tell anyone else—not anyone. This is real personal. I don't know if I should tell you at all, it's so personal," I said.

Janet said, "If people tell you secrets, it means they trust you and like you. I'm your best friend, Natalie. You must like me and you can trust me."

"Well, how come you told me what your sister wrote in her diary?" I asked. "That was secret and personal."

"Yeah, I know," said Janet, "but I only told you because you're my best friend. Besides, my sister's real bratty anyway, and mean too sometimes. I cross my heart and hope to die: I won't tell anyone. Was there a boy in your dream, Natalie? Who was it?"

"Well, sort of," I began. "Do you think..." I paused, then went on quickly. "Do you think Mr. Martin is really old?"

"What do you mean?" she asked, puzzled. "Was he in your dream?"

"Yes, sort of," I said.

"What do you mean, 'sort of'?"

I could tell she was getting impatient. "Do you think girls our age can fall in love?" I asked.

"I guess so, why not?" She said. "You remember that bit in *National Geographic* about the girls in Africa or somewhere who are married by the time they're ten? If they can get married, why can't they fall in love too? Although," she added, "they weren't allowed to choose who they wanted to marry, so maybe they didn't love their husbands. My sister thinks she's in love with her boyfriend and she's only fifteen, but I sure wouldn't fall in love with him. He's a nerd. I asked my mom what it's like to be in love and she said it's too hard to explain, but you'd know when you were in love. You'd be able to tell. What are you getting at anyway? What about your dream and Mr. Martin?"

"You promise you won't laugh and you'll swear to keep it a secret," I said.

"All right! All right! For heaven's sake, I promise."

"I think I'm in love," I said.

89

"You are?" Janet's eyes widened. "With who, is it anybody in school?"

"Yes," I said.

"Well, who, for heaven's sake? Don't keep me in suspense."

"Mr. Martin," I said. There! I'd said it. I'd told my best friend. What a relief!

Janet's mouth had fallen open. She didn't laugh. She just sat there, staring. "Mr. Martin," she stammered. I nodded.

Outside the treehouse the bell rang and Mom called, "Natalie, Janet! Supper's ready. I've got to go now."

"OK, Mom," I yelled. "We're coming. Come on," I said. "Let's get that pizza." I felt great. There was a big load off my mind. Janet was still sitting and staring at me. For once she had nothing to say.

"Natalie!" Mom called. "I've got to go or I'll be late."

I stuck my head out of the treehouse and yelled, "Coming," and started to climb down. I got to the foot of the ladder, but I had to holler at Janet before she appeared in the doorway of the treehouse. My news seemed to have put her into shock. "Come on, let's go," I said.

Mom was standing on the deck in the light from the kitchen's patio door. It was dark outside now. I walked towards Mom with Janet trailing behind me and climbed the steps onto the deck. Mom was all dressed up. "Oh, there you are. I've got to go now. I've just turned off the pizza so it's still nice and warm. I don't think I'll be too late. You'll be OK, won't you?"

"Sure, Mom," I said. "Have a good time."

She bent down, kissed me on the cheek, said, "Bye, Janet," and went quickly down the steps to the garage.

"Come on, Janet," I said. "Let's eat. I'm starving."

We went into the house and hung our jackets in the porch. The warm spicy smell of pepperoni pizza greeted us as we went into the kitchen. We went to the bathroom to wash our hands.

"Does he know?" Janet asked.

"Who?" I said. We dried our hands and went into the kitchen. Mom had left the plates ready by the oven.

"Mr. Martin. Does he know?" Janet went on.

I put on some oven mitts and took the pizza out of the oven. "Er, yes... Well, maybe... I'm not sure. But he will soon."

"What do you mean, he will soon?" she asked.

I started to cut up the pizza. "Well," I said, "he just will." I wasn't absolutely sure Mr. Martin had read my poem yet. Janet helped herself to some pizza. I went to the fridge. "Do you want some milk or more lemonade?" I asked.

"Lemonade," Janet said. "Look, we've got to talk. How do you know you're in love with Mr.

Martin? Do you really have that feeling my mom was talking about and couldn't describe?"

"Yeah, I guess so." I brought the lemonade to the table and poured two glasses.

"Do you feel different? Are you absolutely sure?" she pressed.

"All I know is that if he would wait until I finish school I'd marry him, if he asked me," I said.

"But that's years away," she exclaimed. "Anyway, you can't." She bit off a large piece of pizza and began chewing.

"What do you mean I can't? Is he married or something?" I began to worry.

"No," she mumbled, her mouth full of pizza. "Don't you know?"

"Know what?" I asked.

"Well..." Janet swallowed. "How can you marry him when he's been going out with your mom so much?"

"She's only been meeting him because of the playground," I said.

"Gee, you're dumb," she said. "I'm not supposed to tell you this, it's a secret. At least Mom said I shouldn't say anything to you after I heard her and your mom talking. But I guess I gotta, seeing as how you told me your secret and you're my best friend."

"What is it?" I asked anxiously.

"Well, my mom and your mom were in our

living room the other day when I was home with that bad cold. I was in the kitchen. My mom didn't know I was there until she came into the kitchen to get more coffee. When she saw me she looked annoyed and sent me to my room so I couldn't listen any more. After your mom had gone, she asked me if I had heard what they were talking about. I said sort of, and she said I wasn't supposed to say anything to you or anything at school.''

"Say what?'' I asked.

"Well, your mom and Mr. Martin are going out together. Your mom was talking to my mom about how you might feel about that when I overheard their conversation.''

I hadn't eaten anything while Janet was talking. "You mean, she hasn't been just going to meetings about the playground—they're—they're dating, maybe even in l-lo-?'' I couldn't say it. Janet nodded.

"I know he came here to supper, he's been here a few times, but I thought all the other times were about the playground.''

"Well, they weren't,'' said Janet. "Your mom has been dating Mr. Martin. Where do you think she is tonight, for Pete's sake? Did she tell you who she was going out to supper with?''

"She usually does,'' I said, "but I forgot to ask. I was thinking of something else. Oh no, I've really done it now.''

"Done what?" Janet asked and attacked another huge piece of pizza.

"Well, you know when I said he'd know how I felt about him soon?" I groaned.

"Yeah. Well, what?" Janet's mouth was full again.

"Well, I wrote this dumb poem and put it in his lesson plan book at home time today. He'll have read it by now, and he'll show it to Mom tonight," I wailed.

"Oh yeah?" Janet laughed. "He won't know what to do—wait for you or marry your mom. Of course he could marry your mom now, and then get a divorce and marry you when you leave school."

"Oh shut up!" I said. "Get serious. It isn't funny."

"Sorry," Janet said and bit off another piece of pizza. "But he hasn't read your poem yet."

"What?" I said. "How do you know? Tell me."

"Well..." Janet licked her fingers, taking her time. I could have strangled her, she took so long. "He left the room the same time we did, and when we were getting on the bus I saw him in the parking lot getting into his car. So you see, your poem is probably still in his plan book. He won't read it till Monday morning."

"We've got to get it back," I said.

"Whaddaya mean, 'we'? *We* didn't write it. *You* did. It's your poem," she said.

"Come on," I said, "let's go."

"Go where? Mmm, this pizza is good. If you're not going to eat it, I will." She reached for a piece from my plate. "Go where?" she repeated. "You don't mean to the school, do you?"

"Yes," I said, "we've got to get that poem back before Mr. Martin reads it and thinks I'm a real klutz. And what will Mom think? This is the first time she's gone out with anyone since Dad died and I've messed it up for her. Why didn't she tell me she was keen on Mr. Martin?"

"You were probably blinded by your love for him," Janet giggled. "But maybe your mom wasn't sure if you'd understand, seeing as he's your teacher and everything. She may be just going out with him, but when I heard her talking to Mom, she sounded like it was the real thing for her." Janet went on chewing.

"How can you eat at a time like this?" I snapped. "How would your mother feel if she had a boyfriend and she found out you were trying to steal him away from her?"

"I dunno," Janet said. "But my dad might be upset if he found out my mom had a boyfriend."

I glared at her. "Be serious."

"OK," she said and stopped eating. "What's the worst that can happen? Mr. Martin reads your poem, he gets embarrassed, especially if he reads it when the whole class is sitting there, he tells your mom, and your mom kills you." She started to laugh again.

"Come on, Janet!" I almost started to cry. "I

don't want to mess things up for Mom." Janet finally realized I was serious.

"But how? The school will be locked, and how are we going to get into town anyway? You're not thinking of taking the tractor again, are you? 'Cause if you are, count me out."

"We'll take my bike," I said. I wouldn't dare take the tractor again, especially in the dark. "We'll ride double. You can ride on the seat. Come on, let's go."

"What about Mrs. Stevenson?" Janet asked. "What's she going to do when she finds we're gone? Remember, she's supposed to drop in and check up on us."

"Oh no," I groaned. "Let's leave her a note. We have to get the poem back without anyone knowing."

"What did you say in that poem anyway? Was it real mushy stuff?"

"Sort of," I said. "You know—about love and stuff."

"It's useless, you know. The school will be locked. We won't be able to get in," Janet said.

"Stop saying that. We'll find a way," I said desperately. I found some paper and a pen and printed a note for Mrs. Stevenson after we discussed what to say. It read:

Dear Mrs. Stevenson:
I've taken Natalie and Janet with me to

town. Sorry to have botherd you. I tried to phone, but the line was busy and we had to leave in a bit of a rush as I was late as usual.

Jennifer Webster

We stuck it on the door to the kitchen. I hoped Mrs. Stevenson didn't know Mom's printing and that I hadn't made any spelling mistakes.

CHAPTER TEN

"Come on," I said. We grabbed our jackets and ran out to the tool shed where I kept my bike. Luckily there was a moon, because I knew my headlight was not working. I got my bike out of the shed.

Janet said, "Maybe we'll have to break into the school."

"Oh sure," I said. "How?"

"Take a screwdriver," she said. "It might be useful. I saw a guy on TV break into a place with one once."

Janet held my bike, and I ran back into the shed and grabbed a big screwdriver off the shelf and stuck it inside my jacket.

"Come on," I said, "hop on." Janet climbed onto the seat of my bicycle and I started to pedal down the driveway. I wobbled a lot and Janet hollered once or twice when I zigzagged wildly and nearly hit the ditch. After we had gone about a kilometre I was hot and nearly out of breath. Janet took over and I sat on the seat.

After she had wobbled all over the road for a while she stopped the bike and said, "Sit on the handlebars. I can steer better that way. That's how I give my brother a ride sometimes." I hopped off the seat and onto the handlebars. We started off again. Janet said, "That's better. It's easier to steer." She didn't wobble so much, but it was a bit scary riding on the handlebars, because Janet had to look over my shoulders to see where she was going. A few times I yelled "Keep left," when she seemed headed for the ditch.

We got to the paved road, and I took over the pedalling again while Janet sat on the handlebars. I found it easier, but Janet had to tell me where I was going as she is a bit taller than me and I couldn't see over her very well.

When we got to the first steep hill we got off and walked. We were both hot, even though it was a cool night. One or two cars passed us but we kept well over on the shoulder of the road. We rode on again. It seemed to take ages before we got to the top of the last hill and saw the lights of the town below. Janet sat on the handlebars again, and I was able to coast most of the way downhill.

Luckily the school was just on the edge of town so we wouldn't have to go right downtown. It wouldn't do to meet Mom and Mr. Martin. We'd have too much explaining to do. As we reached the school parking lot the moon went behind a cloud. It was pretty dark except for a light over the main door of the school. I stuck my bike in one of the bike racks and we crept towards the front door.

"OK, now how are we going to get in?" Janet asked.

I thought for a minute. "Maybe the janitor's here. We could ring the bell and say we left something important in the classroom and needed it this weekend." I looked around the parking lot behind us. There were no cars to be seen. "There's no one here," I said. "There aren't any cars. Anyway Mrs. Turner would never believe us, even if she was here." We tried the door, but as we'd suspected, it was locked.

"Come on," I said, "let's walk around and see if we can get in a window."

"They'll be locked too," Janet said, as she followed me around the side of the school. It was pretty dark and scary and we walked along close to the wall. As Janet had said, all the windows were locked. Mr. Martin's room was on the second floor around the back of the school at the far end. We turned the corner of the building and followed the wall.

Partway along there is a kind of courtyard where the wall we were following changed direction, leaving an open area. We sometimes played tetherball there. We were about to cross this area when the moon came out and I glanced to my left.

"Terrific!" I said and stopped so suddenly that Janet bumped into me. "Look at that." I pointed to the one window in the courtyard. It was open.

We ran towards it as silently as possible and peered in. It was very dark inside, but there was a bit of light showing over the classroom door leading to the hallway.

"Whose room is this?" I asked.

"It's Mrs. Sylvester's," Janet said. "I can tell by the perfume. Can't you smell it? Pee-u!" I sniffed. She was right. There was no doubt about it. I'd recognize Mrs. Sylvester's perfume anywhere. All the kids in school called her "Skunk" because it was so strong. Some kids said they nearly fainted when she bent over to help them with math, so they didn't ask for help unless they were really desperate.

"How come this window is open?" I said.

"Who cares," Janet replied. "Maybe Mrs. Sylvester left it open by mistake or maybe the janitor left it open to air out the room or something. Anyway, hurry up. Get in and find that poem. Don't stand here wasting time."

"Give me a leg up," I said. Janet boosted me in the window, and I fell inside and bumped a filing cabinet with a loud bang.

"Sssh," Janet whispered. "Don't make so much noise. I'll wait here and keep watch."

I felt my way along the rows of desks to the

classroom door. My heart was pounding. I opened the door quietly and peered out. The hall seemed quite bright after the darkness of the classroom except where one of the lights over some lockers was out. The lockers were old and were being replaced. The school district's repair crew had been working on them earlier in the day. Mr. Martin's room was up the staircase farther down this hall, past the lockers.

I closed the door behind me and started tiptoeing down the hall. Then I had an awful thought. Suppose our classroom door is locked and I can't get in. Then I had an even worse thought. Suppose the door to Mrs. Sylvester's room locked behind me and I can't get out. I ran back the way I'd come and tried the door. I sighed with relief when I felt the knob turn in my hand. It was unlocked! Mr. Martin's might be too. I didn't know if the classrooms were locked at night or not.

I crept back down the hall past the lockers and reached the foot of the staircase. I looked up into the darkness at the top of the stairs, my heart beating madly. I took a deep breath, grasped the handrail, and then tiptoed quickly up the steps. Halfway up, a stair creaked and scared me, but I went on and reached the top. I hurried to our classroom door. I turned the knob. The door opened. I left the door ajar and went in. I didn't dare switch on the light.

As I walked between two rows of desks towards Mr. Martin's desk, I suddenly heard a hissing sound over by the wall. I froze and held my breath. What was it? I listened, my heart pounding. I relaxed when I realized it was only the heater coming on.

I reached Mr. Martin's desk and found his plan book. There was some light from the moon coming in through the one window by his desk. I opened the plan book, pulled out the envelope with my poem in it, and pushed it into my jacket pocket.

I wanted to run from the room, but I forced myself to walk. I didn't want to trip over anything like Jimmy Chan's gym bag, which was usually on the floor instead of on the shelf. Mr. Martin was always telling him to put it away because he kept tripping over it himself.

I reached the door and closed it quietly behind me. I started tiptoeing down the stairs again and down the hall towards Mrs. Sylvester's room. I was just going past the row of old lockers when a light flared at the far end of the hall, near the front of the school. I froze against the lockers, holding my breath. What was it? Had I been discovered? I stepped behind an open locker door and peered around it.

I could just make out the shapes of two people kneeling on the floor by the door of the secretary's office. They seemed to be wearing ski hats or tuques on their heads. I couldn't see their faces. Who were they? I asked myself, and what were they doing? What were they holding? The light that had flared seemed to be some kind of torch, like the ones welders use. Were they here to fix the door or something? I wondered.

They hadn't seen me, but I couldn't move. If I went forward towards them to get to Mrs. Sylvester's room, they'd see me.

Suddenly I thought, Maybe they're burglars— but what could they want to steal from the secretary's office? The African Children's Relief Fund! That was it. Only today we had brought back our collection boxes and they were probably all stored in the secretary's office. They must have known somehow that the money was being kept in there. They must be trying to burn the lock off the heavy wooden door, I thought.

I was petrified. I didn't know what to do. What if they had guns? I couldn't just jump out and say, "You're under arrest!" The only weapon I had was the screwdriver, which was still stuck inside my jacket. I hardly dared to breathe.

Stay calm, Natalie, I told myself. Think. Slowly a plan formed in my head. I'd wait until they went inside the office, then I'd make a run for Mrs. Sylvester's room. I'd climb out the window where Janet was waiting, and we'd run and phone the police.

Yeah, that's what I'd do. But what about the

poem? How would we explain what we had been doing at the school? I thought some more. We could phone the police without giving our names. That way the crooks would be caught, and Janet and I could cycle back home without anyone knowing we'd been in the school. Yes, that was it. It was perfect. I peered around the locker door again. They were still working on the door to the office.

Crash! I jumped. What was that? Somewhere behind me a door had slammed. It must be the side door of the school, I thought. Someone had just come in and would see me if I stayed there.

I didn't dare look around. The two burglars were on their feet. They'd heard the noise too and were looking down the hall towards me. I bit my lip and slowly squeezed myself inside the old locker. I pressed myself as far back as possible. I didn't dare try closing the door—the burglars and whoever was behind me would see it move.

I heard the sound of feet coming from the direction of the side door, and suddenly there was a shout.

"Hey! What's going on?"

Someone ran past where I was hiding towards the two burglars. I caught a glimpse of him as he passed, and I almost died. It was Mr. Martin.

I peeked through the gap where the door was hinged to the locker. Mr. Martin was running towards the burglars, who looked startled. They just stood up. They seemed about to run, but couldn't make up their minds. They had dropped the burning torch they had been using.

Now Mr. Martin had reached them. I heard him shout something, and he grabbed one of the crooks. I pressed my eye closer to the gap and saw them struggling. Suddenly I saw Mr. Martin go down, hit on the head by something that the other crook had in his hand. I almost screamed. I was about to leap out and make a run for it to get help when one of the two burglars yelled, "Come on, let's get out of here!" They started running down the hall towards me.

I pressed myself into the back of the locker and held my breath again. They were coming closer. Maybe they wouldn't see me. Their footsteps reached the locker, and suddenly there was a crash and a curse. The door of the locker slammed shut, leaving me in darkness. I stifled a scream as the footsteps faded and I heard the outside door shut with a slam. One of the crooks hadn't noticed the open door of my locker and had run into it. But they hadn't seen me and they were gone.

Slowly I let out my breath. I pushed against the door of the locker. It wouldn't move. It must be stuck. Don't panic, I thought. Just give it a good hard push. I tried again. Nothing happened. Somehow it was jammed. I turned my body around slowly to get my back against the door.

There wasn't much room. I pushed and tried to raise my foot behind me to give the door a good kick. But I couldn't bend my knee to raise my foot, so I couldn't kick hard.

What about air? Would I run out of air? Help, somebody...anybody! I had visions of my body being found on Monday in the locker. Maybe Mr. Martin was dead too, I thought. My poem would be found. I could see the headline now in *The Elmwood Bugle*: "Secret Elmwood Elementary Lovers Die in Suicide Pact."

"Oh," I groaned, "I've ruined everything: Mom's love life, her big chance for happiness." The scandal would ruin everything. Even if Mr. Martin wasn't dead, how would I ever explain what he and I were doing in the school at night together? My poem would be found and Mr. Martin would be fired.

I could hardly breathe. I was running out of air. Calm down, Natalie, I said again. I wriggled around to face the door again and saw a faint glimmer of light. I looked up. There was a small grille just above my head in the door of the locker to let air in and, I suppose, to let smells out—like sweaty gym socks or old lunches.

Good, I thought. I'm not going to die. I can breathe. I let out the breath I'd been holding. Now to get out. I pushed again at the door. I yelled and banged my heels and fists against the walls and the door. I had to get out. Maybe I could explain things somehow. No one answered. Janet would never be able to hear me. She must be wondering what has happened to me, I thought. Mr. Martin must be either unconscious or dead. "Oh God, please don't let him be dead," I begged.

I pushed hard against the door and yelled, "Hey, let me out, I'm in here!" I turned sideways. I rocked and banged my shoulder against the door. The door stayed shut and I hurt my shoulder, but I thought I felt something move. I rocked again and I was sure something moved. The next time I gave a bit of a jump and threw all my weight at the door. I was right, something did move—the whole locker. It wasn't bolted to the wall any more.

My world leaned over, and with an awful crash that left my ears ringing, I found myself lying down. It was a pretty hard fall and I felt sore in a few places, but I couldn't move enough to rub them. I was still inside the locker, and worse, the door was on the floor underneath me. I was completely trapped. It was impossible to open the door now, and even the grille was facing the floor. I was in complete darkness.

Now I really began to worry about air. I yelled—screamed would be a better word—and banged my heels and fists against the inside of the locker. Then I listened. Nothing—no sound at all. I screamed again and banged some more.

CHAPTER ELEVEN

"**I**s that you, Natalie? Stop screaming. You're scaring me. What are you doing in there?" I heard the muffled voice of Janet outside the locker.

"Get me out," I yelled.

"Where's the door?" Janet asked. "How did you get in there? I thought you said you left your poem on Mr. Martin's desk, not in a locker."

"I did. I'll explain later, just get me out."

"How?"

"I don't know!" I yelled. "Try!"

"OK. I'll try to turn the locker over," Janet said. I heard her pant and grunt and then she said, "It's no use. You're too heavy. I can't move it. What are we going to do?"

"Is there any other way I can get out?" I yelled. "I'm running out of air."

"Oh no," Janet howled, "don't say that! I'll go and get help."

"No," I said, "don't leave me. Janet," I called. "Janet, are you still there?"

"Yeah," she said, "what can I do?" Her voice now came from the direction of my feet. I kicked at the bottom of the locker in frustration.

"Hey," Janet said, "do that again." I kicked again. "When you did that," Janet said excitedly, "the corner of the bottom moved and I saw your shoe. You won't run out of air. Kick it again."

I kicked again as hard as I could.

Janet said, "There are three screws holding on the bottom. One of them is missing. That's why the bottom moved and I saw your shoe. Have you still got the screwdriver?"

"Yeah," I said, "but it's in my jacket. How do you expect me to hand it to you, you dummy?" I was glad Janet ignored my remark about her being a dummy.

"Can you get it out of your jacket and get it down to your feet?" she asked.

"I'll try," I said. I couldn't move my arms very much but I managed to unzip my jacket and take the screwdriver in my hand. "I have it in my hand," I said. I stretched my hand as far as I could towards my feet, but I could only reach just below my knee because I couldn't sit up. "I can't reach," I yelled.

"Oh no!" Janet hollered. "The school's on fire!"

"What?" I yelled. I pulled the screwdriver back and threw it towards my feet. It's amazing what you can do when your life's at stake.

"Janet," I yelled, "can you see the screwdriver? I have it jammed between my feet."

"No," she said. "I can't. Look, there's a fire at the other end of the hall, and a—a body!" Janet gasped.

"Yeah, I know," I said and pressed even harder against the bottom of the locker.

"What? How do you know?" Janet asked in a horrified voice.

"It's Mr. Martin," I told her. "Some burglars hit him on the head and then took off. They must have started the fire. Quick, go and see if he's OK. Hurry."

I heard Janet's footsteps race down the hall. I had visions of being fried alive in this tin box of a locker. I strained and pressed as hard as I could and wondered how the fire started. I heard Janet return.

"I think he's still alive, but he's unconscious. I couldn't move him by myself—you'll have to help me. The office door is on fire."

"Well, for heaven's sake, get me out. I've got the screwdriver between my feet. Can you see it?" I was desperate.

"Hey! I can see it," she yelled excitedly. "Press a bit harder." I pressed and prayed that it wouldn't slip and fall between my feet underneath me. I felt it wiggle.

"I've got the end of it," Janet said, "but I can't get the handle out, it's too big. Press a bit more."

I pressed. "I've got it," yelled Janet. I felt the screwdriver slip away.

"Stop pressing," Janet called, "I can't move the screw." I heard her grunt. "It won't turn," she yelled.

"Try harder," I yelled back.

She grunted again. "It's moving."

"For Pete's sake, hurry up."

"I've got the screw out. I'll try the next one," she said.

Hurry. Oh please, hurry, I begged silently. I heard her grunt again.

"It's moving, it's coming. Got it!" she yelled. "Press with your feet again. We might be able to bend the bottom back."

I pressed and she got her hands inside the flat metal of the bottom. Between us we bent it back. I felt Janet grab my feet and pull. "Come on," she said. "Help me."

I wriggled, and my feet and legs were out. What if I get stuck, I thought. Oh no, please don't let that happen.

Janet pulled again and I wriggled some more. Why do girls have such big hips? I groaned. This was one time when I wished I was a boy.

"I'm stuck," I yelled.

"Come on, try again. One, two, three, now!" Janet pulled again and I was almost out. One more pull and my shoulders cleared the bottom of the locker. I eased my head out. I was free.

"Oh thanks, Janet, you saved my life." I hugged her.

"Yeah, but look at that fire, and what about Mr. Martin?" Janet pointed.

"Come on," I said. We raced down the hall to where Mr. Martin was lying. Beside him the door of the office was smouldering. The fire had been started by the torch, which was still burning at the bottom of the door where the burglars had dropped it.

"Quick, we've got to move Mr. Martin away from the door. Grab hold of his arms," I cried.

We grabbed Mr. Martin and pulled—thank heavens for polished floors and the fact that he wasn't fat. We dragged him away from the door and I gasped when I saw the small pool of blood. It was now smeared across the floor where we'd dragged him through it.

"He's bleeding!" I cried. Blood was trickling from a cut on the back of his head.

"We've got to get help," Janet said, staring at the blood on the floor. She looked a little pale.

"Look," I shouted, "there's a fire extinguisher. Let's try to put out the fire."

We ran down the hall and lifted the fire extinguisher off the hook on the wall. It was heavy, and it took the two of us to drag it close to the door. The heat was pretty bad.

"We've got to turn that torch off first," I said.

"How?" Janet asked. I reached for it—it was

like the one I'd seen Mom use to fix things around the farm—and felt the heat from the door against my face. I held the torch at arm's length and turned the small knob on the top of the cylinder. The flame flared and got longer. Janet shrieked and I nearly dropped it.

"Wrong way," I said and turned the knob in the opposite direction. The flame died and disappeared with a small pop.

"How do you work this extinguisher?" Janet asked. "The school will burn down if we don't hurry up."

We quickly read the directions on the extinguisher: "Use On Class A Fires Only—Wood/Paper/Textiles—Hold Upright—Push Safety Lock Forward—Squeeze Trigger."

"OK," I said, "quick, help me." I pushed the safety lock forward like it said, and we both grabbed hold of the trigger. We were excited and forgot one thing, but it wasn't mentioned on the instructions so it wasn't really our fault. We forgot to unclip the nozzle from the side of the cylinder, so when we pressed the trigger, foam suddenly shot over the floor.

"Grab the nozzle," I yelled.

Janet grabbed for it and yanked it free from the clip, but she didn't get a good grip on it. The spray of foam shot up the wall, missed the door completely, and sprayed all over the list of kids' names printed on the school's honour roll. She finally got a better grip on the nozzle and managed to point it at the door and I continued to press the trigger. The spray shot all over the door, leaving only smoke and fumes from the foam.

Suddenly there was a hammering at the front door of the school. We both jumped and looked towards the door. I could make out Mom's face peering through the glass. I ran to the door and let her in.

"Natalie! Janet! What are you doing here? What's going on?" Then she coughed as she choked on the smoke and fumes. Suddenly she saw Mr. Martin lying on the floor and rushed to him.

"What happened?" she cried. She knelt beside him and I started to explain about the burglars but Mom only half listened. When she noticed the cut on his head, she said, "Quick, Natalie, go and get some wet paper towels."

I rushed to the bathroom and brought back some towels, and Mom pressed them to the back of Mr. Martin's head.

"Hold this here," she said to me. I pressed my hand on the pad of paper towels while Mom took off her coat and folded it. She placed it under his head to raise it a bit. "I have to call an ambulance. Keep that pad pressed against his head," Mom ordered. She ran to the staff room.

"We should have phoned," Janet said. "How come we didn't think of that?" I shrugged. You can't think of everything, I thought.

Mom came running back and knelt beside Mr. Martin again.

"Is he going to be all right?" I asked.

"I think so," Mom said. She loosened his tie and collar and took over holding the pad to his head. "Now quickly, tell me what happened. Why in heaven's name are you two here, and what caused that fire? I phoned the police and Mr. Stanley, so you'd better have a good explanation."

Janet and I looked at each other. "Well, we came into town to get something I'd left at school," I began. "We found an open window and I climbed in. Mr. Martin came down the hall—he didn't see me, but two robbers were trying to break into the office. They hit Mr. Martin on the head and ran out, and the door caught fire 'cause they were using that torch." I pointed to the torch lying on the floor.

Outside the ambulance arrived, with lights flashing and siren screaming.

Mom said, "You can tell me the rest later. Let them in."

I ran to the door and two ambulance attendants rushed in with a stretcher. They knelt beside Mr. Martin and had a look at him. Mom spoke to them, but I couldn't hear what she said. The woman tied a small bandage around Mr. Martin's head. He stirred and opened his eyes.

"Jennifer." He looked dazed and sounded like

he was drunk. He looked at us. "Janet? Natalie? What's going on?"

Mom squeezed his hand. "It's going to be OK."

A police car, its lights also flashing, arrived, followed by Mr. Stanley's car. Two police constables and Mr. Stanley walked up the side-walk together. Janet and I looked at each other but said nothing. Mom pushed open the door and they came in.

Mr. Stanley looked worried. "Mrs. Webster, how's Mr. Martin?" He hurried over to where Mr. Martin was lying. He had a brief word with the ambulance attendant. One of the constables also spoke to Mr. Martin, then the ambulance attendants lifted him onto the stretcher and covered him with a blanket. Janet held the door open as they carried him to the ambulance. We watched through the door as they drove off again with lights flashing but no siren.

Mr. Stanley turned to Mom. "Mrs. Webster, Janet, Natalie—let's all go into the office. Good heavens! What happened to the door?"

"I don't think we should touch the door right now, sir," one of the constables said. "We might destroy some evidence. Can we go somewhere else?"

"Yes, of course, let's all go to the staff room," Mr. Stanley said. He turned to Mom. "When you phoned you mentioned a break-in, but I didn't realize there was a fire too."

"Whoever was trying to break in," the second constable said, "wasn't very smart. That little torch would never burn that lock off."

Janet and I followed Mr. Stanley, the two police constables, and Mom to the staff room. We went in and everyone sat down except Janet and me, until Mom waved us to a loveseat in the corner. Mr. Stanley introduced Mom and Janet and me to the police, who were introduced as Constable Jones and Constable Watford. Constable Jones took out a notebook and pen, looked at Mom, and said, "Can you tell us exactly what happened, Mrs. Webster?"

Mom explained that Mr. Martin had gone into the school to pick up some tests he wanted to mark over the weekend, leaving her waiting outside in her car. Constable Jones asked what time that was and Mom told him. She went on, "I waited for what seemed to be a long time, then I came to the door to see what was keeping him. That's when I saw Natalie and Janet and a lot of smoke." All eyes turned to look at us, and I felt nervous. "My daughter, Natalie, let me in," Mom went on. "She told me that two burglars had hit Mr. Martin over the head and caused the fire. The two girls had just put it out when they let me in. I saw Mr. Martin on the floor and called an ambulance, then I called you, Mr. Stanley."

"OK," Constable Jones said. "Now, Natalie and Janet, can you please describe what happened?"

I looked at Janet, took a deep breath, and said, "We were outside and saw an open window. I climbed in and saw the burglars and then Mr. Martin came in the side door and saw them, and they had a fight and Mr. Martin got hit over the head. Then the burglars ran out and the door caught fire and—oh, sorry about the wall and the honour roll, Mr. Stanley. I guess we made kind of a mess putting out the fire."

"Now slow down, take your time," Constable Jones said. "Where did you get in?"

I told them about the window in Mrs. Sylvester's room.

"Next time you see an open window, call us first," Constable Watford warned. "You could have been seriously hurt."

"And where were you when Mr. Martin was hit by the burglars?" Constable Jones continued.

"Down the hall," I said.

"Can you show us where?" Constable Watford asked. Constable Jones nodded.

We all walked down the hall, and when we came to the locker lying on the floor, Mr. Stanley said, "These old lockers are being replaced. They must have knocked this one over."

I told the police that I'd hid by the lockers and climbed inside one, and the robbers slammed the door—with me inside—when they ran past. "It fell over while I was trying to get out," I explained. Mom looked startled when I told them this part.

"Did you hurt yourself?" she asked anxiously, looking at me closely for the first time.

"Just some scratches and bruises, I think," I replied sheepishly. Mom sighed and said she'd check me over when we got home.

"And where was Janet?" Constable Jones continued.

"Janet was outside until after the burglars had gone. Then she came and helped me get out of the locker."

"Did you get a good look at them? Can you describe them?"

Constable Jones wrote in his notebook as I said, "They wore ski masks over their faces, but I think they were teenagers. They were wearing jean jackets and jeans. That's all."

"And you didn't see them at all?" he asked Janet.

"No," Janet said in a funny voice. "I came in after the robbers had gone when Natalie called me."

Constable Jones sucked his pen. "So you came in because Natalie needed help. Is that right?"

"Yeah, right," said Janet. Constable Jones closed his notebook and we walked back towards the staff room and sat down again. Constable Jones went to the phone and made a call to the police station.

"I'm not clear on one point," Constable Watford said. "Why were Natalie and Janet at the school? Were they with you, Mrs. Webster?"

Mr. Stanley nodded. "I was wondering the same thing."

Mom looked at us. "No, they were outside and happened to be passing. Could you leave that with me?" she asked. "I'm sure they were just trying to be helpful, and they've had a bit of a shock."

I looked at Mom gratefully.

"Yes, yes, of course," Mr. Stanley said. "I'm only glad nothing happened to them and they had the presence of mind to put out the fire or the whole school might have gone up. Is that all right with you, Constables? I think we should get these girls and Mrs. Webster off home, it's getting late."

Constables Jones and Watford nodded, and Constable Jones said, "I think that's all we need for now, Mrs. Webster, girls. If you would just leave us your phone numbers so that we can get in touch with you, you can be on your way. Thanks for your help."

We said goodbye. Mr. Stanley and the two constables stayed in the school.

Mom took us to the car. She didn't say anything until we were in the car. Then she said, "Before we go home, I'm going to the hospital to see how Eric is. Then I'll want a full explanation." We said nothing as she quickly drove the few blocks to Elmwood Hospital. She parked outside.

"You wait here, both of you. Don't you dare move," she warned. "I won't be long." She got out and closed the car door.

Janet said, "Boy, what an adventure! Are you going to tell your mom about the poem?"

"I guess I'll have to," I said.

"You did get it back, I hope, seeing that we nearly got killed."

"I got it." I patted my jacket.

"Oh, you'd better take this," Janet said. "You may need it in case we ever have to break into school again." She reached inside her jacket and handed me the screwdriver.

"Janet," I gasped, "I'd forgotten all about it. Thank heavens you remembered it. We'd never have been able to explain a screwdriver at the scene of the crime with our fingerprints on it. You're a lifesaver."

Mom wasn't long. "He's going to be fine," she said. "It's a minor concussion." I saw a tear glisten in her eye. So she is in love with him, I thought. I squeezed her hand and she squeezed mine back.

As we started for home again, Mom said, "Oh heavens, I completely forgot. What about Mrs. Stevenson? What will she have thought when she went to the house tonight and found you two missing? She'll be frantic."

"It's OK, Mom," I said. "We left her a note."

"Good," said Mom. "I'm glad to hear you were

at least responsible enough to do that, but heaven knows why you went to the school in the first place. I don't think I could cope with an explanation tonight—let's leave it till tomorrow. I've had enough excitement for one night." Mom's relief over the fact that Mr. Martin was going to be OK had softened some of her anger.

I was worried about making her mad again. We had just reached the edge of town, not far from the school, when I said, "Oh, Mom. I'm sorry, but we forgot something outside the school."

"Outside?" Mom jammed on the brakes and looked ready to explode. "Oh, Natalie," she groaned. "Not the tractor again."

"No," I said quickly, "my bike."

Mom sighed with relief and said, "Well, we might as well pick it up now. We don't want it stolen." She drove back to the school and put my bike in the trunk. Mr. Stanley's car and the police car were still outside.

When we got home Mom said, "OK, you two, I'll make some hot chocolate and then it's off to bed. You must be exhausted. I know I am." She looked at all my sore spots and said they didn't seem too serious. I could tell I was going to get some nice purple-green bruises on the side that I fell on, though.

As we sat at the table drinking our hot chocolate Mom said, "By the way, I see I spelled 'bothered' wrong in the note I left for Mrs.

Stevenson. It should be b-o-t-h-e-r-e-d, not b-o-t-h-e-r-d," she smiled.

"I guess I was in a rush. Sorry, Mom," I said.

Later when Janet and I were in bed in my room, just before we fell asleep, Janet asked, "Will you do me a favour, Natalie?"

"What?" I said.

"If you ever fall in love again, don't tell me about it."

"OK," I yawned.

CHAPTER TWELVE

We slept until ten the next morning, and when we got up, Mom was in the kitchen. "OK, you sleepyheads, what do you want for breakfast? Waffles and bacon, or pancakes and bacon?"

"Waffles and bacon, please," I said. "OK, Janet?"

"Mmm. Yeah, great," Janet said.

While Mom mixed the batter for the waffles, she said, "I phoned the hospital and Mr. Martin is going to be fine. He'll be out of hospital tomorrow."

"I'm glad," I said.

"Me too," said Janet.

"I need to have a long talk with you, Natalie. I've phoned Janet's mom, and I'm going to have to take you home after lunch, Janet. I hope you won't mind too much, but I want to have a kind of private talk with Natalie. I should have done it before. I hope you understand."

"Sure, Mrs. Webster. That's fine," Janet said. "I know what you mean." She looked at me and grinned.

"OK, set the table, Natalie, and let's have breakfast," Mom said briskly. "Orange or grapefruit juice?"

After breakfast we played Janet's Bruce Springsteen record and watched some TV. We didn't talk much about what had happened, but I wondered how to explain things to Mom.

Janet said, "Don't worry. Anyone who can make waffles like your mom must be real nice." Janet had eaten four for breakfast.

After lunch we took Janet home, and before she got out of the car she whispered, "Good luck. I'll phone you tonight."

Mom was silent on the way home. When we got there she said, "I'll put on the kettle and we'll have some tea." She seemed nervous.

When the tea was made and poured, Mom took my hand and said, "I've got a confession to make, Natalie. You remember the meetings I had about the playground? Well, only some were about the playground. You see, I went out with Eric a few times as well. I really like him, but I didn't know if you'd understand, since he's your teacher. I wasn't sure of my own feelings myself. I am now, though." She stopped talking and looked into my eyes. "I think I'm in love with him," she went on. "I hope you won't be upset. I should have said something before. I suppose I wasn't really being honest with you. I apologize for that—I should have been."

"It's OK, Mom," I said. "I know. I understand. I know how you feel."

"You do? Oh, that's wonderful," she said and hugged me.

"I've got a confession too," I said. "I thought I was in love with Mr. Martin." I told her about the poem then, and how we'd gone to the school to get it back. Mom hadn't said anything about our escapade of last night. She seemed more concerned about how I'd feel about her and Mr. Martin.

When I finished telling her the story, she hugged me again and said, "Oh Natalie, he's a nice man. Anyone could fall in love with him, but I hope we're not going to fight over him." She smiled and I smiled back.

"No, Mom, he's all yours. I don't think it's the real thing any more. You were more worried about him than I was when he was hurt. I saw the way you looked at him—I know you love him."

Mom said, "I guess you've had what you'd call a crush on him—sort of puppy love. You'll grow out of it."

"What did you say, Mom?" I asked. "I thought you said 'guppy love.'"

We looked at each other, then we both began to laugh.

That night Janet phoned. "How did things go?" she asked.

"Great. I guess I'm not really in love with Mr. Martin after all, but my mom is. Don't say anything at school to the other kids. Remember you promised."

"Yeah, I know I did. It's a good thing you got your poem back, though."

"Yeah," I lied. I didn't have the heart to tell her that when I went to put the envelope with my poem in it in the bottom drawer of my bureau, I discovered that I had the wrong envelope. Inside it was a note from Jason Hopkins's mother to Mr. Martin, asking him to excuse Jason for being absent, because of a bad cold. My poem was still in Mr. Martin's plan book. Janet would kill me if she knew we'd gone through all that trouble for nothing.

CHAPTER THIRTEEN

On Monday Mr. Martin was back at school. He was late coming into class and we were all in our desks. He had a small bandage on the back of his head, and lots of kids wanted to know what had happened to him. "I bumped into something," was all he said. His eyes twinkled and he looked up and smiled at me and Janet when he said it. Then the kids asked if he knew what had happened to the office door. They had all been talking about it when I got to school.

"There was a bit of a fire, nothing very serious," Mr. Martin said. He began to call the roll. Janet and I looked at each other and said nothing. I knew Janet was dying to tell everyone, but I had sworn her to secrecy.

Shortly after class started, Mr. Martin was called to the office over the PA. When he left the room, all the kids started talking about the door. Jennifer Mason said she'd heard that someone had broken into the school and tried to burn it down and that Mr. Martin had saved the school. That really got them going. I looked at Janet, and she looked like she was going to correct Jennifer Mason, until I shook my head and frowned at her.

Mr. Martin came back in then and said, "Natalie and Janet, you're to go to the office. It's OK," he smiled.

We looked at each other and went out the door together and down the hall.

"Now what?" Janet asked. "Do you think it's the police again?"

"I hope not," I said.

It was a reporter from *The Elmwood Bugle*, and Mr. Stanley introduced us as the two girls who had saved the school. Mr. Stanley said, "I've already told Mr. Pringle all about what happened, but he wants to ask you one or two questions and take your picture for the paper."

Mr. Pringle said to me, "Haven't I seen you somewhere before?"

I shook my head and said, "I don't think so." Then I realized that I'd seen his name on the report in the *Bugle* about the bees. I hoped he didn't remember me, or he might write something in the paper about the bee disaster again. I wanted to forget that completely.

He apparently didn't remember where he'd seen me, because he only asked a few questions about the fire. They were easy questions, not like the ones the police asked. He asked us if we were scared at the time and how we felt about it now. He said he'd got most of the story from Mr. Stanley. I was glad he had talked to him first and we didn't have to give any details. Mr. Pringle then stood us close together and took our picture. He said it would be in the *Bugle* on Wednesday.

We went back to class and all the kids stared at us curiously. At recess Mr. Martin asked Janet and me to stay behind when the other kids went out.

He said, "I'd like to thank you two for what you did. You probably saved my life."

Janet and I both looked embarrassed and said, "It's OK."

"Well," he said, "thanks again. I was very glad you were there."

He didn't mention my poem, and I felt sure he must have read it by now.

We went outside then and a lot of the kids asked, "Are you in trouble or something?"

We said no, but Janet smirked and couldn't resist saying, "But don't forget to read the *Bugle* on Wednesday."

At home time, when most of the kids were getting their lunch kits and coats, Mr. Martin quietly said to me, "I think this is yours, Natalie. I think you left it on my desk." It was my poem, and the envelope was still sealed. He hadn't read it.

I said, "Thanks," and smiled gratefully. I

131

realized then that Mom must have phoned him about it.

When I got home, Mom had a surprise for me. "Mr. Stanley phoned to tell me that the school board wants to make a special presentation to you and Janet. We have been invited, along with Janet's mom, to a special lunch on Friday."

On Wednesday, when *The Elmwood Bugle* came out, the headline on the front page said, "Disaster Averted—Girls Save School." I wasn't quite sure what "averted" meant, but Mom told me it meant prevented. There was a slightly blurred picture of Janet and me. The article underneath said that the fire in the school had apparently been caused by burglars. Mr. Martin, a teacher, had surprised the two crooks, who had knocked him unconscious and fled. We had seen the fire and climbed in the window left open by the burglars. We found Mr. Martin and put out the fire. The article went on to say that the school board was going to honour us at a special presentation on Friday.

Next day in school, a few of the kids brought the newspaper article, and all the kids kept asking us questions. We only answered the ones we wanted to, and Janet made up a few things that weren't really true. In class Mr. Martin admitted his part in the event and praised us for what we'd done. Janet and I sat there grinning from ear to ear the whole time.

Kevin Windslow and Billy Pinchback were disappointed. They complained, "You should have let the school burn down. We would have given you a reward." I just stuck out my tongue at them.

CHAPTER FOURTEEN

On Friday at noon Mom and Mrs. Sullivan picked up Janet and me at school and drove us to the school district office. All of the school board members were there. Mrs. Bompas was wearing an even shorter dress than usual. She beamed at us, so I guess she had forgiven me for the bees.

We all went to the King's Castle Restaurant. Mr. Martin and Mr. Stanley arrived there soon after us. Mr. Cranshaw said we could have anything we liked on the menu, so Janet and I ordered double cheeseburgers.

Mr. Pringle from the *Bugle* came in, carrying his camera. Mr. Cranshaw rose to his feet and tapped his drinking glass with his fork to get everyone's attention. He cleared his throat, peered at a card in his hand, and began, "We are here today to honour two young girls, whose quick thinking saved one of our schools from disaster. On behalf of the Board of Trustees of Elmwood School District, it gives me great pleasure to award these cheques to..." He peered at the card in his hand again. "Er...Janet Sullivan and, er..." He had more trouble with my name. He squinted at the card and Mrs. Bompas, who was sitting beside him, prompted him. Mr. Cranshaw leaned towards her to catch her words, but he mustn't have heard her clearly because he went on, "And to Napoli Webster." Everyone clapped.

Mr. Pringle took our pictures again for the *Bugle* when Janet and I shook hands with Mr. Cranshaw, as he presented each of us with a cheque for fifty dollars. I was pleased to see that my name was spelled right on the cheque anyway, so I wouldn't have any trouble cashing it.

Mrs. Bompas then got to her feet. "I have a very special announcement to make, and I think this is a good time to make it," she beamed. "Most of the people concerned are here. It gives me great pleasure to announce that the school board has voted to provide five thousand dollars towards Elmwood Elementary School's new adventure playground." Mom's face flushed with pleasure. Janet and I cheered, and Mr. Martin and Mr. Stanley applauded loudly.

As the lunch ended, Mr. Cranshaw looked at his watch and said, "Girls, you're going to be a little late getting back to school, but I'm sure Mr. Stanley and Mr. Martin will excuse you on this occasion." His eyes twinkled as everyone chuckled. As we rose to leave, everyone shook our hands—all, that is, except Mrs. Bompas. She insisted on giving Janet and me a big hug, pressing us against her Dolly Partons before we could escape.

CHAPTER FIFTEEN

I'm glad the Christmas holidays are finally here. There's just been too much excitement this past term. Mr. Martin—I still call him Mr. Martin in school—is going to come for Christmas dinner, and I'm glad about that. I think he and Mom may get married next summer after school is out, and I'm glad about that too. What I mean is, I'm glad about him marrying Mom and also that they are waiting till summer. It would be a bit embarrassing to go to my teacher's wedding during school term, especially when my teacher is marrying my mom.

They started on "Mom's playground" a short while ago. They got a bit of work done, and they're going to finish it in the spring when the snow melts.

I still have my poem in the bottom drawer of my bureau. I'm going to keep it. After all, it's the first love poem I ever wrote, and I think it's a good one. And you never know when I may need it again.

A new boy came into our class just before Christmas, and Janet has taken a fancy to him. His name is Frederick Fortune. Janet said she got a love note from him, but I haven't seen it. She also said she dreams about him, so it could be the real thing.

I said, "It's probably only a crush—probably guppy love."

More Good Books

Maggie and Me
Ted Staunton

Poor Cyril! Without Maggie life would be a lot easier,
but it would also be a lot more boring. MAGGIE
AND ME — a collection of five funny stories starring
Cyril and his best friend Maggie, the Greenapple Street
Genius. No matter what they do, they seem to be in
trouble.

Ted Staunton wanted to be a cowboy when he was
small, but somehow he became a writer instead. He is
also a musician and will perform his songs for anyone
who wants to listen. The author of *Puddleman*, *Taking
Care of Crumley* (also starring Cyril and Maggie) and
Simon's Surprise, he is married and lives in Toronto.

Kids Can Press

More Good Books

Could Dracula Live in Woodford?
Mary Howarth

Gulping, Jennie leaned into the doorway and tried to
see into the darkness. "I can't see anything," she
whispered.

Go in a few steps, I'm not making it up.

Jennie looked anxiously at Beth. "Will you come
with me?"

She nodded. Holding hands, they stepped over the
threshold into the silent house. In the dim light, from
a far wall, two enormous eyes stared at them — dead
eyes — expressionless and unblinking.

Kids Can Press